THE HOLY SPIRIT IN THE CHRISTIAN LIFE

THE HOLY SPIRIT IN THE CHRISTIAN LIFE

W. CURRY MAVIS

BAKER BOOK HOUSE
Grand Rapids, Michigan

ISBN: 0-8010-6010-9
Printed in the United States of America

 Scripture quotations are from the Revised Standard Version unless otherwise specified.

Contents

Introduction

Many Christians today are eager to know more about the way the Holy Spirit works in their lives. They believe that it is as important today for Christians to be acquainted with the Holy Spirit's work as it was for the twelve disciples to be acquainted with the work of Jesus in Galilee. They perceive that the character of their Christian lives depends heavily on how well they comprehend what He wishes to do for them.

In response to this contemporary Christian quest, this book undertakes to help believers understand more fully the nature of the Holy Spirit's presence in our lives. It emphasizes Biblical teachings that deal with the power of the Spirit of God in human life. It also gives attention to the human response to the divine presence.

I have drawn upon both theological and psychological resources in seeking to describe the Christian life; upon theology when dealing with the Spirit's influence and power in our lives; and upon valid psychological resources when discussing our responses to the Spirit of God.

In the first section of the book we shall look at the nature of the Holy Spirit's influence in the *emotional aspects* of the Christian life. Many Christians have found that their greatest personal problems come about when the "negative" emotions cause them to behave in un-Christian ways. They look upon that triad of emotions—anger, guilt, and anxiety—as destroyers of the spiritual life. They sense deeply their need of the Spirit's help in this matter, for it seems often that "the intellect is stilled, and the emotions alone perform their . . . involuntary functions." Christians sometimes feel like a distraught man who exclaimed, "We are not men of reason, we are creatures of emotion." Furthermore, we shall see how the Holy Spirit strengthens three positive emotions in life—love, peace, and joy. These emotions are most basic in our lives, and they are constructive and life building.

Second, we shall look at the presence and power of the Holy Spirit in the Christian's *devotional life.* The devotional life of the believer is important because it is both a basis for and an index of the quality of his spiritual life. We offer the Spirit a good opportunity to guide and help us in times of prayer and worship, for it is then that we are most open and ready to respond to His presence. The Spirit strengthens us as we are open in heart and mind, expectant, and ready to respond.

In the third section of this study, we shall look at how the Holy Spirit helps us to be *effective Christian witnesses* in both life and work. The Spirit transforms the quality of our personal conduct, and He enhances our abilities for Christian service. He does these things by working deeply in the interior lives of Christians, imbuing them with His enabling presence. His holy presence establishes an interior basis for righteous living and effective service.

The Holy Spirit's presence is essential in our lives because He enables us to live dynamically for Christ. Personal spiritual decline sets in when we neglect His presence. Without His sustaining power, we move from spiritual reality to barren religious ritual and, then, to hollow religious role playing.

The work of the Spirit is both broad and deep. He reaches into every part of our lives, and He strengthens every aspect of them. He leads us into a knowledge of Christian truth. He enables us to do God's will as He guides and strengthens us in times of personal decision. He fortifies us against the wiles of the devil in times of temptation. His presence gives us spiritual initiative and energy that help us to overcome the debilitating effects of apathy. His indwelling provides a bracing Christian atmosphere that enables holy aspirations to arise. His grace makes it possible for us to fulfill sacred objectives. He cleanses our hearts from the heavy drag of sin. He grants us gifts and divine enablements so that we may witness to others. He enables us to live in Christian victory.

Part 1

The Holy Spirit Transforms Our Emotional Lives

1 The Spirit Helps Us with Anger

"My tendency to anger is the greatest problem in my Christian life," said a sincere parishioner to his pastor as they talked together about personal Christian experience in the quiet of the pastor's study. "I could be a victorious Christian," the parishioner said, "if it were not for the spiritual setbacks that I have in the vexing circumstances of life."

The tendency to be angry when provoked is not limited to the layman. Recently a minister who had reached the highest level of leadership in his denomination confided to a friend that the dominant personal problems in his Christian life had arisen from his disposition to irritability and hostile feelings.

Every Christian should know the nature of human anger and understand the moral and spiritual significance of angry feelings. There are those Christians who have given up on the problem of personal anger because they have come to believe it is so deeply rooted in human nature that they can do nothing more than try to inhibit it. These people need to see that there is divine therapy for this problem.

Paul viewed hostile-mindedness as a primary characteristic of the "natural man." In Galatians 5:17–21 he named specifically fifteen works of the flesh, and of this number, seven are related definitely to hostility and contention: enmity, strife, jealousy, anger, dissension, party spirit, and envy.

Paul recognized, however, that there is a qualitative spiritual and moral difference between angry feelings and angry behavior. He said to the Ephesians, "If you are angry, do not let anger lead you into sin" (Eph. 4:26 NEB). A few centuries before the time of Christ, the Greek language used one word, *thumos,* to suggest angry feelings and another word, *orgē,* to suggest angry behavior. This distinction was not made in the Greek language of the New Testament. We must determine from the context whether the words used for anger suggest angry feelings or angry demeanor.

This chapter looks at the subject of anger feelings analytically by dealing first with the basic nature of human anger and with some of the factors conditioning it. Next, we shall see how the Holy Spirit wishes to help us with the problem. Finally, we shall notice the constructive uses of anger in the spiritual life.

The Nature of Human Anger

Anger is an emotional reaction that is sometimes aroused when a person is interfered with, threatened, injured, or simply frustrated. It is composed of four basic elements. First, there is a feeling of unpleasantness. Second, there are changes in the glandular system. As noradrenalin is poured into the blood stream, there is a higher pulse rate, higher blood pressure, higher respiration, and lower rate of digestion. Third, there are exterior bodily changes including skin flushing, change of voice, and dilation of the eye pupils. And finally, there are impulses of aggression with tendencies to overcome the frustrating person or object.

Frustration is a primary cause of anger. The human organism often responds autonomically to frustration. The adrenal glands, quite apart from volition, pour a secretion into the blood stream that causes feelings of anger and aggression. Infants, who lack the ability to discriminate between right and wrong, sometimes become angry when the free movements of their hands or feet are hindered. In so responding, their reactions are prototypes of adult behavior when frustrated.

From another viewpoint, anger in the human personality is a God-given capacity to be used to overcome evil. Men living in earlier periods found it useful in overcoming physical dangers. When threatened—e.g., by predatory animals—the human organism inwardly mobilized itself for a maximum expenditure of energy in overcoming the threat. There are constructive uses for anger in our present age.

Conditioning Factors of Anger

It is axiomatic that anger is a greater problem for some people than for others. This is true even among Christians. There are a number of reasons for this.

Temperament is one, affecting both the readiness and intensity of hostile feelings and actions. Persons of the choleric temperament have inherited dispositions to be quick and intense in anger. They may be highly sensitive to situations of frustration, and their glandular activities cause them to be angry. On the other hand, there are persons of the sanguine temperament who on the basis of the chemistry of their bodies have little difficulty with anger, even before Christian conversion. Being organically predisposed to be happy and optimistic, they usually overlook frustrating situations without anger.

Again, childhood and adolescent experiences often contribute to the making of angry adults. If children are not taught to look for constructive solutions in frustrating situations, they may grow up with a habit of concentrating attention only on frustrations with an ever-increasing hostility. Persons who had temper tantrums in childhood sometimes continue in adulthood to give uninhibited expression to their anger. It seems that intense and often-repeated emotions may leave a residue that develops into personal emotional attitudes. When acted out often, emotions may become a habit. Furthermore, persons who were rigidly thwarted in carrying out their motives in childhood are often angry persons, particularly if in early life they repressed their anger.

Furthermore, maladjusted persons frequently have strong tendencies toward anger, for frustration tolerance is often low in them. The well-adjusted person normally has fewer provocations to anger, but the maladjusted person lives in a world of personal threats. The anxiety-ridden person is threatened always by dangers, many of which are of his own imagination. The person loaded with inferiority feelings encounters many frustrations and situations in which his ego and a sense of his essential worth are threatened. The personally insecure person might fight many psychological skirmishes in needless self-defense.

Finally, life's vocations and professions differ in the number of personally frustrating situations they present. The driver of a school bus loaded with uninhibited high-school students has more annoyances than a research student hidden away in a library. And a theological-seminary teacher is subject to fewer frustrations than a teacher of lively junior-high-school youngsters.

The Spirit's Therapy for Anger

The therapy of the Spirit is seen in His work in the mind and heart of the believer as He enriches and strengthens the interior life. His work is in the spiritual-psychological areas of life and surely not in the physiological. He enables mature Christians to have inner spiritual resources so that they do not feel defeated and deeply frustrated in difficult situations. The problem of anger is diminished as the occasions for a sense of frustration are lessened.

Forgiveness. The Holy Spirit aids the Christian to diminish his impulses to anger by helping him to become forgiving of others because he himself has been forgiven by God. The person who will not forgive others lives in a psychological-spiritual climate in which personal resentments and anger flourish.

"The forgiven become forgiving" is a constant principle of the Christian life, and this is demonstrated in the experience of converts. Before one's conversion one is ill prepared psychologically to grant others that which he himself has not received from God.

After conversion one no longer relies heavily on counterattack in situations of injury and frustration; the convert forgives for he knows he has been forgiven. In many cases his own forgiveness brings a deeper understanding of himself, and thus of others, and he is able to forgive others for he knows about the inner dynamics that motivate men to injure their fellows. Forgiveness becomes a new method to the convert in handling injustices. He believes that when injurious actions start on the part of an "enemy," acts of understanding and kindness should be initiated by him.

The matter of timing is important when one comes into frustrating interpersonal stresses. Jesus said, "Agree with thine adversary quickly. . . ." (Matt. 5:25 ASV). This is psychologically sound, for continued thought on a frustrating matter in interpersonal relationships almost always causes irritation or anger. Paul urged a quick solution to frustrations lest the devil get the upper hand. He told the Ephesians to refrain from thinking about them. "Do not let [the] sunset find you still nursing it; leave no loop-hole for the devil" (Eph. 4:27 NEB).

God's Spirit gives us a readiness to forgive others by enabling us to accept their frailties as we remember that God accepts us with all of our inadequacies. We recognize that we too wrong people by our thoughtlessness and self-interests. Thus, not asking for special privileges, we are willing to let other people be human.

The Christian's practice of forgiving others, by the help of the Holy Spirit, is a type of spiritual cleansing that rids the heart of resentments, bitterness, and negative feelings toward others. If these feelings remain in the life of the Christian, they become a seed bed for hostile impulses. When forgiveness is deep, there is no residue of bitterness left and we are not predisposed to have hostile feelings toward another who has wronged us. Shallow forgiveness of others permits tendencies to hostility to remain in the heart, but deep forgiveness of others washes them away.

A realistic self-image. The Holy Spirit helps to deliver us from hostile impulses by enabling us to have a basically accurate and humble view of ourselves. Paul viewed this as a constant law of the Christian life based on the presence of God in the believer. "For by the grace given to me I bid every one among you not to think of himself more highly than he ought to think, but to think with sober judgment, each according to the measure of faith which God has assigned him" (Rom. 12:3). Self-enhancement or pride is a chronic cause of frustration. Chaucer, an astute observer of human behavior, said that pride is "the general root of ire."

The person who has strong motives to aggrandize himself meets with numerous occasions that may arouse anger. He puts himself in unrealistic competition with others, trying to gain overly ambitious objectives. When he becomes frustrated, his glands pour more noradrenalin into the blood stream and his organism is set for defense. A humble and realistic view of self reduces the occasions for such preparations on the part of the organism.

The matter of self-image becomes especially difficult in competitive societies in which social recognition and vocational success depend heavily on one's personal qualifications. Thus every person is motivated to appear as socially attractive and vocationally superior. Persons strive to build their self-images along these lines. This means that every man with an overly high self-image is threatened psychologically and spiritually.

The Spirit of God helps the Christian to have a basically true self-image. The maturing Christian looks at himself with growing objectivity, seeing more clearly his areas of weakness. He gives up what Karen Horney called his "pride system," and so his autonomic nervous system has fewer occasions to prepare itself for defense.

Spiritual strength. The Holy Spirit helps us meet frustrations by giving us a sense of spiritual adequacy and strength. Our ability to handle frustration depends heavily on a sense of our strength. We are likely to feel disturbed when we feel that we are losing control of a situation. Those persons with deep inferiority feelings face a most difficult situation in this respect because they feel inadequate to meet many life situations and because their frustration tolerance is low. Alfred Adler went so far as to say, "We must interpret a bad temper as a sign of an inferiority complex."

Paul remained tranquil in situations that were most frustrating. A sense of divine strength caused him "to take pleasure in" threats, reproaches, and dangers. "And he [the Lord] said unto me, My grace is sufficient for thee: for my strength is made perfect in weakness." Paul responded to the divine voice, "Most gladly therefore will I rather glory in my infirmities, that the power of Christ may rest upon me. Therefore I take pleasure in infirmities, in reproaches, in necessities, in persecutions, in distresses for Christ's sake: for when I am weak, then am I strong" (II Cor. 12:9, 10 ASV). In referring to the deprivations and persecutions that he was experiencing, he said, "I can do all things through Christ which strengtheneth me" (Phil. 4:13 ASV).

Here is one of the miracles of the Christian life! The spirit enables us to have joy instead of anger in life's frustrating situations. The sense of God-given strength makes difficult situations challenging and gives us new verve to encounter them.

Authentic love. Paul shows that love is the best therapy for anger because it cuts the roots of angry impulses. "Love is patient, and kind: love is not jealous or boastful; it is not arrogant or rude. Love does not insist on its own way; it is not irritable or resentful; it does not rejoice at wrong, but rejoices in the right. Love bears all things, believes all things, hopes all things, endures all things" (I Cor. 13:4–7). There are five prominent elements of love in Paul's statement that relate directly to angry impulses.

"Love is patient" (v. 4). The New Testament word for patience means most basically "to keep good tempered under provocation." It means also to be longsuffering in bearing the offenses and injuries of others, to be slow to avenge one's self and slow to retaliate, verbally or otherwise. Patience is most important in avoiding anger, for much anger arises out of our lack of inner fortitude to meet the annoyances of life.

"Love is not . . . boastful, it is not arrogant or rude" (vv. 4, 5). Love cuts the impulses of much anger by preventing us from making boastful claims about ourselves that must be defended; it saves us from feeling elevated over others.

"Love does not insist on its own way" (v. 5). Love removes much of the frustration that causes anger by helping us to have open minds and relaxed attitudes as to how things should be done. The spontaneity and creativity of love frees us from old stereotypes and rigid patterns and enables us to do things in the way other people wish, without feeling frustrated and rejected.

Love "is not irritable or resentful" (v. 5). Love is an effective therapy for anger because it increases one's toleration of annoyances. One ceases to be difficult to please because love of God and of others makes us less aware of our own personal whims. Moreover, love does away with resentments; it does not keep track of the wrongs one receives.

"Love bears all things . . . hopes all things" (v. 7). Love does not give us inner fortitude through a Pollyanna attitude of irrepressible optimism, the attitude that everything is good. Instead, love gives us mettle through faith and hope. Love makes us strong because it "believes all things . . . hopes all things" (v. 7). Love lifts our eyes from the hectic present to the long-range view, which reveals the solution of present vexing problems by God's grace.

A love of others, as we love ourselves, is a good therapy for ego-defensive anger. Having a genuine love of others, we recognize that they too have unique personalities with various areas of strength and weakness, and we remember that fact. John Rutty, an eighteenth-century Quaker physician, noted in his diary: "Vexed at a servant, but the passion shall not rise, I hope. Why should I be disquieted at the peccadilloes of others."

The Positive Use of Anger

Human anger in itself is not evil, for it may be used either righteously or unrighteously. Someone has said, "Anger is one of the sinews of the soul; he who lacks it has a maimed mind." Anger has both creative and redemptive uses.

Using anger creatively. Christians normally have a sense of shame when they become angry, and they have strong tendencies to deny and repress distraught feelings. The first step in handling angry feelings creatively is to acknowledge them. This step cannot be by-passed; denial and repression of angry feelings lead to guilt and anxiety, to a loss of self-knowledge, and to a callow heart. But to acknowledge angry feelings, we must have the help of God.

Again, the Holy Spirit helps us to make angry feelings creative, or really reconstructive, by using the sense of guilt occasioned by anger to motivate us to greater self-perception. Numerous specific causes for anger may be found when we look deeply within ourselves. We may see, for instance, that our angry feelings come from our immaturity. We may come to see ourselves much as pampered children who readily resist everything that interferes with us. Again, for example, we may see that our inferiority feelings become occasions for a sense of frustration or that an overly high self-image occasions an aggressive defense of our phantom self. Increased self-perception helps us pray more wisely.

Furthermore, God's Spirit motivates us to examine the environment in which we live so as to discover and to remove as many frustrating situations as possible. Setting the alarm clock earlier, for instance, may reduce the early-morning haste and the frustration of getting to work late.

More importantly, the Spirit helps us diminish annoyances and frustrations that come out of interpersonal relationships. He enables us to understand better the people who annoy us as we take the initiative to know them more thoroughly. "Annoying people" often become agreeable people when we come to know why they act and react as they do.

Using anger redemptively. Jesus incarnated the righteous anger of God in His own holy person, and He used it redemptively. When the Pharisees showed little compassion for persons who were afflicted, being more concerned about keeping the Sabbath in a rigid and legalistic manner, Jesus looked at them "with anger, grieved at their hardness of heart" (Mark 3:5). When His disciples were so insensitive to the worth of children that they rebuked the parents for bringing their children to Jesus, "He was indignant" (Mark 10:14).

Anger can help to deliver one from nonchalance and passivity. The intense concern that one shows about righteousness when indignant becomes a positive witness to morally casual people. Moreover, anger is accompanied by a driving power that enables one to overcome obstacles of evil. Martin Luther said, "I never work better than when I am inspired by anger. When I am angry, I can write, pray, and preach well, for my whole temperament is quickened, my understanding sharpened, and all mundane vexations and temptations depart."

There have been times when God needed men with a large potential for anger to work out His will in the world. Luther was such a man. No sanguine man could have led the Reformation. Perhaps Erasmus saw even more incisively than did Luther the need for reform in the Roman church, but being sanguine in temperament, instead of rebelling against a monstrous evil he wrote a book, *In Praise of Folly,* in which he satirized and criticized folly in high ecclesiastical places. On the other hand, Luther, being of choleric temperament and led by the Spirit, attacked the evils for the sake of righteousness.

Every Christian, however, should take care that he does not rationalize his ego-defensive anger as righteous, for it is difficult to distinguish between sinful anger and righteous indignation. John Wesley believed that such a distinction could be made only by the help of God's Holy Spirit. Wesley wrote to a Mrs. Bennis, leader of a group of women's bands, that "there is an anger which is not sinful, a disgust at sin which is often attended with much commotion of the animal spirits; and I doubt whether we can well distinguish this from sinful anger but by the light of heaven."[1]

---

1. *The Letters of the Rev. John Wesley,* ed. John Telford, 8 vols. (London: Epworth, 1931), 5:243.

Conclusion

The Holy Spirit brings about a deep renewal within us that relates to anger. The cleansing of the Holy Spirit is both gradual and immediate. For instance, W. Ferguson, an early Methodist convert, trusted Christ for a deep inward change and "in a moment . . . I felt every kind and degree of anger and resentment quite taken out of my heart. My pride was gone. . . . I was crucified to the world, to all of its honors and profits, and to all of its pleasures and comforts."[2] Ferguson's language may sound extravagant to many contemporary readers, but the principle of immediate spiritual cleansing is solidly based; it is God's response to the Christian's act of faith.

The Holy Spirit also cleanses in gradual ways. He leads us into a deeper understanding of ourselves, and He helps us grasp more fully the riches of His grace. He creates within us a sense of dissatisfaction about our lives, and He helps us trust Him for specific advances in the spiritual life. Saints are made by the continued working of the Spirit of God in the inner life.

The choleric and impulsive Peter had a deep spiritual cleansing at Pentecost (Acts 15:8, 9), and he finally became a man of great patience in a day when Christians were persecuted. He had come to the place where he could follow the example of Christ: "When he was reviled, he did not revile in return; when he suffered he did not threaten; but he trusted to him who judges justly" (cf. I Peter 2:18–25). The mature apostle who said those words was a different person from the one he was when, in Gethsemane on the night of Jesus' arrest, he cut off the ear of Malchus.

Questions for Discussion

1. There are several synonyms for *anger.* What are the basic meanings of *anger, rage, indignation, animosity, wrath,* and *irritation?*
2. Ernest M. Ligon stated that three kinds of circumstances may cause human anger: (1) "blocked behav-

---

2. *The Arminian Magazine* 5 (1793): 348.

ior" (frustration), when we are prevented from doing what we want to do; (2) "wounded vanity," when others think less highly of us than we think they should; and (3) "injustices to ourselves and to our friends."[3] Are there other kinds of life situations that provoke human anger? If so, what are they?

3. Do you believe that the physiological (or glandular) basis for anger in times of frustration is similar to the physiological basis for fear in times of danger?
4. Do you believe that feelings of aggression against a person who frustrates you are usually grounded in anger? Is it this element that most often leads one to sin?
5. Do you believe that persons with a sense of insecurity or inferiority are more prone to anger than persons who feel secure and basically adequate?
6. The Bible speaks of God as angry. What were some of the situations that caused divine wrath? Consider Exod. 4:10–17; Num. 11:11; Judg. 2:12–14; I Kings 14:15; Isa. 1:4.
7. The Gospels suggest that Jesus showed no anger when deserted by His disciples, tormented by Roman soldiers, and crucified on the cross. What does this say to His followers?
8. Should a Christian feel anger when he sees injustices done to helpless people? May he be righteously angry when injustices are done to himself?
9. What are some situations today at which Christians may be righteously indignant?
10. How valuable is the Christian witness of bearing injustices with patience and tranquility?
11. Do you believe that a basis for adult anger is often laid in childhood? What are some things parents should do when their children become angry?
12. What did James mean when he said that "the anger of man does not work the righteousness of God"? See James 1:19–21.

---

3. *The Psychology of Christian Personality* (New York: Macmillan, 1935), p. 269.

2 The Spirit Resolves Our Guilt

Mankind has a continuing concern about human guilt. Throughout history men have built altars, constructed temples, commissioned men to be priests, and developed sacrificial systems in an effort to assuage their guilt. The problem of guilt remains today, and men continue to build altars and temples for the "handling" of sin. It has been said that all the problems of the world can be reduced to two: the existence of sin and the freeing of man from its power and pollution.

Repressed guilt becomes the source of anxiety and of irrational fears. As William Wordsworth said, "From the body of a guilty deed a thousand ghostly fears and haunting thoughts proceed." Repressed guilt produces such negative traits as anger, rebellion, a deadening of the conscience, an inability to recognize one's faults, and a growing dominance of the aggressive tendencies. Guilt brings about irritation, inflexibility, and insecurity. It makes people who were once confident become timorous. Repressed guilt may intimidate the brave and debilitate the strong.

The Holy Spirit meets man at the point of his deepest

need in helping him to resolve his sense of real guilt. We must have divine assistance in handling our personal guilt because we cannot make ourselves righteous. Psychotherapy, as a healing art, has no way to enable persons to get rid of their sins; God alone can do that. The Holy Spirit gives believers a sense of "realized forgiveness," and nothing short of this will meet man's deep desire for a right relationship with His Maker.

The Spirit Takes Away Real Guilt

Real guilt is the mental-emotional state in which we recognize that we have sinned or have violated some ethical or religious principle which we endorse personally. Feelings of guilt occur normally when a person sins against God or man. In real guilt we see the wrong that we have done and we feel regret and sorrow for it. Real guilt is characterized normally by feelings of personal blame, moral or spiritual inferiority, unworthiness, and anxiety.

Feelings of real guilt are also experienced, as the existential psychologists have pointed out, when we become concerned that we have not actualized ourselves (by the grace of God) as moral and spiritual persons. This type of guilt arises primarily out of a recognition of what we are and not from what we have done. It is the regret and sorrow we feel when we look at the inferior state of our moral and spiritual selves.

The Holy Spirit brings about a sense of real guilt in the minds of people because this is necessary to their personal redemption. We cannot be saved from sin unless we both see our sins and care about them. Even God cannot save the spiritually nonchalant; morally casual people never enter the kingdom of God. The Holy Spirit prepares people to enter a new personal life, said Jesus, by convicting them "of sin and of righteousness and of judgment" (John 16:8). Soren Kierkegaard wrote, "To become a Christian presupposes the consciousness of oneself as a sinner, and a desire to become a Christian, for any other reason is not only madness but a crime of . . . high treason."[1] He said that when there is no emphasis on consciousness of sin, Christianity becomes mere sentimentality.

The Holy Spirit is both the creator of guilt feelings and the reliever of them. Thomas Walsh, an eighteenth-century convert, experienced deep guilt feelings for an extended period before the Spirit of God induced him to trust Christ: "He [the Holy Spirit] kindled in my soul earnest desires toward God. There was a tenderness in my heart. It began to warm and dissolve after it was broken by the law, and scorched by the wrath of God; and to be a little comforted and encouraged. . . . Light began to spring up within my mind; I saw at length not my guilt only, but likewise the all-sufficiency of Christ and his atonement. . . . I had strong hope that God would be merciful to my unrighteousness, and blot out my sins for his name's sake. I could, as it were, see the promise and pardon held forth before me, though as yet I was unable to lay hold of them. . . . There was kindled in my soul a still more vehement thirst for Christ. . . . And now . . . the clear day began to shine, and the Lord, who 'is rich in mercy,' visited me with his salvation."[2]

The Holy Spirit leads spiritually concerned people through a meaningful experience that frees them from a burden of real guilt and gives them an assurance of personal forgiveness. The first element of this experience is repentance.

The Spirit helps to change our minds about sin. The Holy Spirit helps us to rethink and mentally relive morally unsatisfactory experiences in our lives. As the Spirit accompanies our minds into the past, He gives us light to see the true nature of our actions. As we stand apart from these personal deeds, separated from them by time, our perspective is more objective than when we committed the deeds,

---

1. In Reider Thomte, *Kierkegaard's Philosophy of Religion* (Princeton: Princeton University, 1948), p. 163.

2. In Thomas Jackson, *The Lives of Early Methodist Preachers,* 3rd ed., 6 vols. (London: Wesleyan Conference, 1872), 3:57–59.

and we can better evaluate our deeds against the truth of God's Word. The Holy Spirit at such moments helps us to feel sorrow for our wrongdoing and to cease being personally defensive. This promotes a change of mind about our moral and spiritual failures, or repentance. Without the Spirit's presence we cherish our sins instead of hating them, we tend to deny our wrongdoing, to project it to others, to repress and conceal it, or to rationalize it; we try to resolve our guilt by denying personal responsibility for our sins, blaming instead our lack of knowledge, our instinctual urges, our environment, or the devil.

Repentance is characterized by a new openness toward one's self, an openness that is essential to release from guilt. This clarifies perception, removing distortions caused by the shadows of self-concealment. It is as if the doors and shutters of a tightly closed old house are suddenly opened. New insights and attitudes fill the opened personality as surely as light and fresh air fill the opened house. The repenting one sees more clearly the quality of his inner life; no longer does he grope in the shadows of guilt. The inner self breathes the clean air that has displaced the guilt-laden atmosphere.

The insight into self that is attained in repentance is as

important in spiritual therapy as in psychotherapy. Perhaps every person has a deep wish to see himself as he is and to become *actually* what he is *potentially.* Carl R. Rogers believes that the central questions for every person are: "Who am I, *really?* How can I get in touch with this real self, underlying all my surface behavior? How can I become myself?"[3] On the other hand, man wishes deeply to appear good and strong. "Each of us," wrote Albert Camus, "insists on being innocent at any cost, even if he has to accuse the whole human race and heaven itself."[4]

The Holy Spirit enables us, in repentance, to accept the truth about ourselves. We cease to maintain a pretense of goodness and stop using defense mechanisms with God

---

3. "What It Means to Become a Person," in *The Self,* ed. Clark E. Moustakas (New York: Harper and Row, 1956), p. 196.

4. *The Fall* (New York: Knopf, 1957), p. 81.

because God knows the intents of our hearts. We are afraid to deny our sins lest God look upon us as liars. A sense of the divine presence helps us to be morally and spiritually honest.

The Spirit enables us to acknowledge our sins. Jesus' parable of the prodigal son portrays every person's return to God from the "far country" of guilt. The prodigal confessed his sin to his father, saying, "I have sinned, against God and against you; I am no longer fit to be called your son" (Luke 15:21 NEB). The father accepted the son's confession, restored the father-son relationship, and had the festivities begin (Luke 15:22).

Confession is verbal repentance; it is implemented penitence; it is repentance in action. Confession is the penitent's verbal farewell to, and renunciation of, sins that have plagued his life. He declares his commitment to a new way of life. Confession of sins is a second step in the resolution of guilt problems. A genuine change of mind in repentance prepares the way for confession as the new inner attitudes, sentiments, and ideas seek expression. The emerging new self feels deeply that it must now disclaim the facades, hypocrisies, and sins that once characterized it.

The repentant one spontaneously shares with others his new aspirations, sentiments, and purposes because they are deeply meaningful to him. He wishes to tell of the deep joy of his new perspective on life as surely as people delight to tell about a newly purchased home.

Confession must accompany repentance if repentance is to be meaningful. Repentance without confession will leave the penitent worse off than he was before if his good intentions are stillborn. The law of the spiritual life requires an acknowledgment of one's past sins and an affirmation of new intentions.

It seems that the need for confession is written into the very nature of human existence. Carl Jung said that refusal to confess one's sins makes one a moral exile, but confession throws one "into the arms of humanity, at last freed from the burden of moral exile." If a man refuses to confess his wrongdoing, "an impenetrable wall shuts him from the living experience of feeling himself a man among men."[5]

The Spirit gives us faith in Christ. Paul said that personal faith in Christ brings freedom from sin and guilt: "There is therefore now no condemnation for those who are in Christ Jesus. For the law of the Spirit of life has set me free from the law of sin and death" (Rom. 8:1, 2). Again, Paul said that freedom from guilt comes as a gift from God through faith in Christ: ". . . since all have sinned and fall short of the glory of God, they are justified by his grace as a gift, through the redemption which is in Christ Jesus, whom God put forward as an expiation by his blood, to be received by faith" (Rom. 3:23–25). Paul emphasized that God forgives human sin only on the basis of faith. We "who know that a man is not justified by works of the law but through faith in Jesus Christ, even we have believed in Christ Jesus, in order to be justified by faith in Christ, and not by the works of the law, because by the works of the law shall no one be justified" (Gal. 2:16).[6]

Paul recognized that the human race has sought to be free of guilt by doing good works, by keeping the Old Testament law or some other moral code. This method has always failed to resolve guilt because people never know if they have done enough good deeds to "make up" for their evil deeds, and because morally perceptive persons question if such a system exists. They feel ill-equipped to barter with the Almighty. They recognize their failure to do many of the "Thou shalt's" and their transgression of many of the "Thou shalt not's." They feel hopelessly indebted to God. In their best moments they recognize that there is no moral residue from the good deeds that can pay for their evil deeds, for at their religious best they are doing only what God commanded.

---

5. *Modern Man in Search of a Soul* (London: Paul, Trench, and Trubner, n.d.), p. 40.

6. The terms *justified* and *justification* represent a broad theological concept, derived from law, which includes the element of divine forgiveness.

Nathan Bangs, a Christian minister in early America, described his conversion: "Christ was then exhibited to my mind as having 'fulfilled the law' . . . 'bearing my sins in his own body on the tree'; so that I, receiving Him by faith, need not bear them any longer myself. This view humbled me to the dust. At the same time I felt a gracious power to rely upon his atoning merits by simple faith. Instantly I felt that my sins were cancelled for Christ's sake. . . ."[7]

The Spirit makes forgiveness real to us. "Realized forgiveness" is God's remedy for actual guilt. When applied to divine-human relationships, "realized forgiveness" comes about through faith in Christ and is characterized by an awareness that God, for Christ's sake, has released us from our burden of sin.

Some of the basic Biblical words for forgiveness suggest a release from the burden of sin. One Old Testament term has the primary meaning of "lightness, lifting up," suggesting the release one feels when a heavy burden is removed from one's shoulders. Other Old Testament terms may be translated "to cover," "to wipe away," or "to pardon." The most basic New Testament word for forgiveness is *aphiēmi,* and it suggests most specifically the ideas of "sending away" or "remitting." In divine-human relationships, the New Testament concept of forgiveness is seen in God's act of removing one's actual guilt and of restoring that one back into a relationship to Him, free from the guilt that had estranged him from the divine presence. John Bunyan depicted the central idea of divine forgiveness in *The Pilgrim's Progress.* As Christian looked at the cross of Christ in faith, he lost his heavy burden of guilt and became "glad and lightsome, and said with a merry heart, 'He [Christ] hath given me rest, by his sorrow, and life, and death.' "

"Realized forgiveness" is a personal awareness that we have been forgiven. It is often called Christian assurance. It is a conscious recognition, both rational and intuitive, that God has pardoned our transgressions.

---

7. In A. H. Tuttle, *Nathan Bangs* (New York: Eaton and Mains, 1909), pp. 34, 35.

The Holy Spirit uses numerous means to bring about this inner confidence of divine forgiveness, but the most basic one is the Bible. He enables us to identify with great Biblical statements of assurance, and He helps us to see that they apply to us. Moreover, He gives us inner peace and a sense of freedom from condemnation (Rom. 8:1). "Therefore, since we are justified by faith, we have peace with God through our Lord Jesus Christ" (Rom. 5:1). He takes away the old guilty attitudes of estrangement toward God and helps us feel that we belong to God's family. "For you did not receive the spirit of slavery to fall back into fear, but you have received the spirit of sonship. When we cry, 'Abba! Father!' it is the Spirit himself bearing witness with our spirits that we are children of God" (Rom. 8:15, 16). John Wesley described his own heart-warming experience like this: "I felt I did trust in Christ, in Christ alone for my salvation; and an assurance was given me, that he had taken away *my* sins, even *mine,* and saved me from the law of sin and wrath."[8]

The Spirit Gives Insight into Pseudoguilt

Pseudoguilt is false or exaggerated feelings of personal failure. The wrongdoing is often obscure, nebulous, or exaggerated. For those Christians who find it difficult to accept divine forgiveness and to feel accepted by Christ, pseudoguilt is an important problem.

A discussion of the deep unconscious sources of pseudoguilt is beyond the scope of this book, but we cannot fail to discuss some aspects of this subject, for some Christians who are basically well adjusted experience unnecessary guilt feelings. The Holy Spirit does not leave them frustrated and desolate; He brings guidance, insight, and strength to them.

The Spirit aids the immature. Some believers feel guilty when they look at older and more mature Christians and become aware of their lack of spiritual development. They

---

8. *Works,* 14 vols. (New York: Mason and Lane, 1840), 3:74.

fail to distinguish between normal immaturity and arrested spiritual growth. The Holy Spirit helps them to make this distinction and to see that they are not blameworthy for immaturity per se. He makes their concept of a deeper Christian life motivate them to grow spiritually.

The Spirit gives emotional perspective. Again, some Christians feel intermittent guilt because they overemphasize the importance of personal feelings. They think they are forgiven when they have joy and peace, but they fear they are not when they feel discouraged. From a practical viewpoint, they equate divine approval with positive emotions and divine disapproval with negative emotions. The Holy Spirit helps such persons see that divine approval rests not upon such an unstable basis as one's emotions but upon one's faith in Christ and upon God's faithfulness.

The Spirit saves from legalism. Moreover, those who view the Christian life primarily as a matter of doing right deeds and avoiding wrong deeds normally live with intermittent or even chronic guilt feelings. They believe that one ought to live by the rules, but the rules become so numerous and complex that one cannot help but break some of them. These Christians tend to view all rules as of equal consequence and to feel as guilty over breaking an ethical peccadillo as over committing a major offense. Karen Horney pointed out that there is a "tyranny of the shoulds," and if one undertakes to appraise the quality of one's life on his observance of all the "shoulds," he cannot help but feel guilty. The possibilities of doing good are so extensive that one can never be sure that he has done enough not to feel guilty. The Holy Spirit shows openhearted believers that their relationship with Christ rests upon a living faith in Him and not upon their works, that salvation is a gift from God and is not earned by human effort. The Spirit helps duty-driven disciples to see that Christ seeks both good works and love. Love to Christ is the dynamic that produces Christian victory.

The Spirit saves from moral rigidity. Persons who find it difficult to sense the divine forgiveness, for one reason or another, have usually had unfortunate childhood experiences. Those who were brought up in a forbidding home atmosphere, characterized by accusation, blame, and condemnation, often have exaggerated guilt feelings. There is generally a close relationship between these feelings and anxious fears that one is not meeting the expectations of others. The Holy Spirit helps openminded people see the causes of their exaggerated guilt as they use the Bible, worship, counseling, and many other means as therapeutic resources. He helps the guilty Christian grow in insight and grace until he finds release from the heavy burden of pseudoguilt.

Conclusion

The origin and development of religions, apart from divine revelation, show that the human psyche has a deep need to be free from guilt, and that continues to be a central need for people today. We still want to be related to God, to realize the divinely given privilege of God's pardon. Jesus came to earth to make this possible. He was named *Jesus* because "he will save his people from their sins" (Matt. 1:21). Having been forgiven, the believer is freed by the Holy Spirit from guilt feelings.

Christianity is distinguished by its emphasis upon inwardness. The Holy Spirit internalizes in the human heart both the great truths of the faith and the work of God in man. The sense of having been forgiven is an important result of the presence of God's Spirit in our hearts. Samuel Wesley, father of John, referred in part to assured forgiveness when on his deathbed he said, "The inward witness, Son, the inward witness—this is the proof, the strongest proof of Christianity."[9]

---

9. In W. J. Townsend, H. B. Workman, and George Eayrs, eds., *A New History of Methodism,* 2 vols. (London: Hodder and Stoughton, 1909), 1:168.

Questions for Discussion

1. Do you think that a sense of guilt is a primary problem to people today?
2. How important is the work of the Holy Spirit in convicting persons "of sin and of righteousness and of judgment" (see John 16:7–15)?
3. In what sense is God-given repentance a preparation for divine forgiveness? In what sense is it a result of divine forgiveness?
4. Does genuine repentance always have in it a sincere intention to live a new life by God's grace?
5. In what sense is Spirit-inspired confession a preparation for divine forgiveness?
6. In what ways does confession of our sins unite us with our fellow men?
7. Do you think all Christians have a sense of "realized forgiveness"? If not, why?
8. What spiritual means has God provided to assure us of His forgiveness?
9. Distinguish between real guilt feelings and pseudoguilt feelings. Can we distinguish them in our own experience? If so, how?
10. What personality types are most likely to have a sense of pseudoguilt? Is it helpful usually for such persons to rely only on divine forgiveness for relief? If not, what should they do?
11. How can Christians help fellow believers who have a pronounced sense of false guilt?

3 The Spirit Diminishes Our Anxiety

Anxiety in normal people is primarily a religious problem. Its cause is a lack of personal spiritual vitality, and its cure is a greater use of Christian resources. Many Christians are far more successful in reducing anxiety by using basic spiritual means than by trying to deal with such causes as unfavorable childhood conditioning, poor environment, the pressure of competition, and the complexity of daily living.

Anxiety is an emotional state in which we have exaggerated fears of being overwhelmed by a danger, losing a cherished value, or failing to achieve an objective. Normal anxiety is an "emotional experience with a sense of uncertainty and helplessness."

Every thoughtful Christian wishes to be as free from extravagant fears as possible because he knows that they hinder his Christian effectiveness. They make him weak when he should be strong, doubtful when he should be confident. They diminish his witness for Christ because they reveal a lack of faith. They may even cause him, like Peter, to deny his Lord.

The Bible calls for people to be free from anxiety. Jesus

said, "Do not be anxious about your life, what you shall eat or what you shall drink, nor about your body, what you shall put on" (Matt. 6:25). Paul said to the Philippians, "Have no anxiety about anything, but in everything by prayer and supplication with thanksgiving let your requests be made known to God" (Phil. 4:6). Peter exhorted hard-pressed and persecuted Christians to "cast all of your anxieties on him [God] , for he cares about you" (I Peter 5:7).

The Holy Spirit is the great divine therapist for anxiety in normal people. He creates within us a deep dissatisfaction with our little faith and thus about our anxieties. He leads us to see the reasons for our anxieties, enables us to use the resources God has provided for us, helps us perceive in the Bible great statements about God's care for His children, and makes these relevant and alive to us.

The Spiritual Significance of Anxiety

Anxiety, like the climate, may influence every part of our lives. It beclouds our view of the divine resources that make victorious life possible. It disables us from making affirma-

tive decisions that are in God's will. It normally creates negative and hostile attitudes that prevent us from having joy and peace. Finally, anxiety hinders our prayer lives and lessens our faith by weakening our relationship with God.

Anxiety hinders perception. Anxiety affects perception in a number of debilitating ways. The anxious person concentrates his attention on the threatening and negative aspects of his situation and loses sight of the long-range positive values. He sees reality in a distorted form. Anxiety normally prevents the promises of divine help in the Bible from shining forth and obscures even the power and greatness of God.

It is a well-recognized fact that one sees things as *one is* and not as things are. The pessimist sees pessimistic things, the optimist optimistic things. Every man projects his feelings on the things he sees, tending to interpret them in line with his own attitudes and emotions. Anxious people distort perception by projecting their unrealistic fears on the situations they observe.

Anxiety hinders decision making. It causes us to overemphasize the negative facts of life. It diminishes our ability to concentrate. It constantly distracts us, preventing us from looking thoroughly at all the elements of a situation. At other times our decisions are conditioned by too many "if's" and "maybe's." Driven by doubts and uncertainties, we often delay decisions so long that no good decision can be made.

Moreover, anxiety predisposes us to carry out decisions in a weak and timid way, with numerous reexaminations of the decision as we start to implement it. We hesitate as we seek to move forward. Our energy for constructive life diminished by anxiety, we carry out our decisions without vitality. There is frequently a close relationship between apathy and anxiety, with the former masking an exaggerated fear.

Anxiety causes hostility. Anxiety often causes hostility, and hostility is often a source of anxiety, as Horney has emphasized. Several elements in the anxiety syndrome have the potential to arouse hostility. Anxiety, like fear, calls for defensive actions, and the human organism has inherent tendencies to prepare for "fight or flight" as a means of self-preservation. Anxiety arises out of a sense of frustration, and frustration often gives rise to anger and aggression. Finally, the one who is anxious often feels alienated from others, particularly persons who "threaten" him, and there seems to be a tendency in human personality to be hostile to "aliens."

Anxiety weakens divine-human relationships. Anxiety tends to destroy the very foundation of our Christian lives. It strikes at the heart of our relationship to God by diminishing our trust in Him and in His ability to care for us. We then increase our management of our lives, like the young boy who, fearing an insufficiency in his well-established and affluent home, left it to go out into the world to provide for himself.

Anxiety tends to destroy the sense of relationship with God, the sense of the presence of God in the world, which are basic to the Christian life. It makes practicing deists of us, believing that God exists but viewing Him much as an absentee landlord who gives all His attention to other parts of the universe. It denies that God's world is benevolent and friendly and suggests that we are at the mercy of arbitrary and impersonal laws.

Anxiety destroys the finest things in the religious life. It obscures the promises of God and destroys the spirit of devotion, prayer, and worship. It lessens Christian aspiration, and the spiritual life loses some of its appeal. Anxiety makes people spiritually tired, and a tired Christian is like a tired soldier sent out on an important mission.

Anxiety, said Soren Kierkegaard, "is the psychological condition that precedes sin."[1] It infects confidence with worry, joy with apprehension, and peace with agitation, removing some of the Christian's strongest fortifications against sin. Kierkegaard said that anxiety "makes the individual impotent, and the first sin always occurs in impotence."[2]

The Causes of Anxiety

We shall observe three basic causes of human anxiety in this section. The first is human finiteness. There are things in our physical and social environments that are beyond our control, and these things may cause us to be apprehensive. The second is guilt. And the third is the sense of personal unfulfillment we develop when we see how we have failed to actualize the potential God has given us.

Anxiety and human finiteness. Many people of Jesus' generation had chronic anxiety because they felt uncertain about meeting the daily problems of providing food and

---

1. *The Concept of Dread* (Princeton: Princeton University, 1944), p. 82.

2. Ibid., p. xii.

clothing. Food, for example, depended so largely upon the sunshine and rain, and these people, being finite, had no way to control the weather.

Man's infinitude normally contributes to his anxiety. He meets situations that he does not understand and encounters forces he cannot control. His understanding of the present is limited, and his knowledge of the future is nil. He is unable to control many of the forces of life. He cannot have health by choosing it, and he cannot negate death. He makes the basic human choices with limited knowledge, and his social conditioning often predisposes him to make the wrong choices.

Basic anxiety is augmented by a sense of aloneness and helplessness in an unfriendly world. Unless a person has great faith in God, he has no place to turn when he faces the humanly uncontrollable forces. He cannot help but be anxious.

Anxiety and guilt. Actual guilt is a primary cause of anxiety because it creates in our minds feelings of isolation and estrangement from God. We come to fear divine retribution, even when we sense a need for punishment. The relationship between guilt and anxiety appeared early in our racial history; after Adam and Eve disobeyed God, they felt guilty, afraid, and anxious, hiding from God when they heard His voice.

Real guilt estranges one not only from God but also from one's fellow man. The guilty one feels unworthy and unaccepted. He feels estranged from the one whom he has wronged and fears counterattack from him. Thus he prepares to defend himself, and in the process he increases his feelings of hostility and in turn his anxiety. Hostility augments and strengthens anxiety.

Moreover, real guilt makes us anxious concerning our real selves. We know that sinful deeds come from our real selves and that they are not mere moral accidents. We come to see that the actual self is not the idealized self. We come to fear the interior motivations that are not subject to conscious control, and this moral insecurity becomes a seed bed for anxiety.

All of these feelings of isolation and estrangement are contrary to our essential nature, and they produce extravagant fears. We were created for relationship, not isolation; for fellowship, not alienation. Some psychotherapists believe that contemporary man needs most a "relief from a sense of isolation and estrangement."

Anxiety and human emptiness. Much anxiety is caused by a sense of emptiness that comes from a lack of spiritual meaning in our lives. Man has a spiritual disposition, and when the mind is empty of concepts of enduring worth, it becomes restive, much as the body becomes hungry when it lacks food. The eternal spirit in man, looking beyond the present life, becomes anxious if it sees no eternal values. The writer of Ecclesiastes opened his book with the declaration that earthly things cannot satisfy the longings of the eternal spirit in man: "Vanity of vanities. . . . All is vanity" (Eccles. 1:2).

Some contemporary psychologists say that many people are living in an "existential vacuum"—their lives are not motivated by a commanding purpose. They sense a deep void in their lives; they do not feel challenged; they lack long-term goals. Having lost a sense of ultimate meaning in their lives, they suffer from inner frustration. Leo Tolstoi experienced something very much like this. Despite his riches, high social position, and wide range of earthly interests, "I felt that the ground on which I stood was crumbling, that there was nothing for me to stand on, that what I had been living for was nothing, that I had no reason for living. . . ."[3]

The Spirit's Therapy for Anxiety

Jesus taught that there are two ways of life and that a person may choose which he will follow (Matt. 6:19–34). First, there is the way of anxiety, as practiced by the

3. *The Living Thoughts of Tolstoi*, ed. Stefan Zweig (New York: Longmans and Green, 1939), p. 3.

Gentiles of Jesus' day. Not knowing about the heavenly Father's concern for His children, they lived in fear. Second, there is the way of faith in an infinite God who is concerned for all men. Faith in God meets the basic problems of anxiety in normal people. It brings divine resources into our lives to supplement our finitude. It cancels our real guilt and gives us a fraternal relationship to God. It fills human emptiness with Christian purposes and eternal meanings.

Finite man draws on infinite resources. The Holy Spirit helps us as believers when we are anxious and afraid that we cannot meet the demands of ordinary life. He reminds us, for instance, of Jesus' words about God's loving care for His children, and He makes these words convincing and compelling to openhearted believers. The Spirit shows us that the best antidote for anxiety concerning the uncertain future is to trust in the unchanging God, and He helps us believe personally that the heavenly Father is active in the world and that He feeds the birds and clothes the lilies in regal beauty. This results in a deep sense of stability and a diminishing of anxiety. The Spirit helps us have spiritual poise in difficult times, preventing us from meeting threatening situations impulsively or, on the other hand, from surrendering supinely to them. He helps us accept our human limitations without being crippled by a sense of inferiority or discouragement. He gives us a spirit of prayer and inspires a strong faith that God will guide us in life's difficult situations, that God will strengthen us so we can be at our best. He enables us to have the experience of which William James wrote: "It is but giving your little private convulsive self a rest, and finding that a greater self is there."[4]

Christian biography is luminous with the accounts of devout persons who accepted the help of the Holy Spirit in handling their anxiety. Frances R. Havergal, disposed in early life toward anxiety, later said: "All touch of worry, care, anxiety, and fidget about anything earthly or heavenly

---

4. *Varieties of Religious Experience* (London: Longmans and Green, 1902), p. 111.

is gone. Jesus takes it all, and the rest of faith is more perfect and uninterrupted than I imagined it possible for anyone of my nervous, highstrung temperament to enjoy."[5] John Wesley, anxiety-prone in young manhood, said in his later years: "By the grace of God I never fret, I repine at nothing; I am discontented with nothing. I see God sitting upon his throne and ruling all things well. . . . Ten thousand cares of various kinds are no more weight or burden to my mind than ten thousand hairs are to my head."[6] Our final and most important example is Habakkuk. The ancient prophet lived in an agriculturally oriented society, and he knew that hunger, suffering, and even death resulted when crops failed. However, he was so much aware of the presence of God that he found joy and strength instead of anxiety.

> *Though the fig tree do not blossom,*
> *nor fruit be on the vines,*
> *the produce of the olive fail*
> *and the fields yield no food,*
> *the flock be cut off from the fold*
> *and there be no herd in the stalls,*
> *Yet I will rejoice in the Lord,*
> *I will joy in the God of my salvation.*
> *God, the Lord, is my strength;*
> *he makes my feet like hinds' feet,*
> *he makes me tread upon my high places.*
> (Hab. 3:17–19)

The Spirit delivers from guilt-ridden anxiety. By making us aware of divine forgiveness, the Holy Spirit diminishes our anxiety and frees us from our slavish fear of and hostility toward God. The vicious cycle of anxiety and hostility is broken. The Spirit's cleansing of the memory of real guilt frees us from the spiritual contamination of our past lives.

---

5. In James Mudge, *The Saintly Calling* (Cincinnati: Jennings and Graham, 1905), pp. 176, 177.

6. Ibid., p. 45.

A sense of divine forgiveness also helps us relate to others. The matter of being accepted by and of accepting others is important, for insecure and stressful interpersonal relationships cause much anxiety. Once able to accept ourselves, we are able to accept others. We can adopt new attitudes toward those who create in us feelings of hostility and anxiety because we no longer need to defend ourselves.

The Spirit gives meaning to human life. The Holy Spirit shows us, through the message of Jesus, that we must center our lives in spiritual purposes inasmuch as human personality is essentially spiritual. He reinforces Jesus' twofold call to a spiritually integrated life: "Do not lay up for yourselves treasures on earth . . . but seek first God's kingdom and his righteousness" (Matt. 6:19–33). Jesus taught that anxiety is inevitable for the person whose primary interests are earthly things—whether his livelihood, his possessions, or his personal status and recognition.

That integration of life around spiritual principles is an antidote to anxious concern is seen clearly from the meaning of *merimna,* the New Testament term for "anxiety": "drawn in different directions." The word suggests a state of disorganization in which conflicting interests produce frustration and stress. The anxious life is filled with numerous contrary objectives and impulses. Jesus called for an integration of interests. The new spiritual purpose reduces the number of stress points, where the lightning can strike. Moreover, it becomes a frame of reference to guide all perceptions and actions, making perplexing facts understandable.

Jesus taught that every man should live for something bigger than himself. "But seek ye first the kingdom of God, and his righteousness. . . ." (Matt. 6:33 ASV). Life turns in on itself when one's main purpose is to save his own life. "He that saveth his own life shall lose it" is a sound psychological as well as religious principle. Some profound existentialists have pointed out that physical life itself is not fully satisfying and meaningful until one consciously values something else more dearly than one values one's own life.

Victor Frankl told of a woman who, realizing the emptiness of her life, seriously considered suicide. Finally, with the help of the Holy Spirit, she sensed that God had a purpose for her life. This insight breathed into her fainting spirit a breath of fresh air. She then said, "God wants something of me. I don't exactly know what; it is up to me to find out. Sometimes I could shout for joy—life is beautiful, beautiful, beautiful, beautiful."

By centering his life in spiritual values, Paul became free of all anxiety about his own death; it actually became a favorable option to him. During the latter part of his life he wrote, "For to me to live is Christ, and to die is gain. . . . I am hard pressed between the two. My desire is to depart and be with Christ, for that is far better. But to remain in the flesh is more necessary on your account" (Phil. 1:21, 23, 24).

Conclusion

The Holy Spirit helps openhearted Christians overcome

their anxieties by giving them a sense of the divine presence. Thus, the Christian feels that the universe is hospitable and friendly, not hostile, and he is related, by divine grace, to the eternal God. The psalmist David said in Psalm 23 that he was not anxious about personal needs (v. 1) nor about peril and death (v. 4), because God was with him. He believed that his real pursuers were "goodness and mercy" (v. 6), not the evildoers of the world.

The Holy Spirit also helps Christians overcome anxiety by giving them an inner strength that enables them to cope with life's problems. Paul said of his ability to cope with difficult situations in life, "I can do all things through Christ which strengtheneth me" (Phil. 4:13 ASV). He exhorted the Philippians, "Have no anxiety about anything, but in everything by prayer and supplication with thanksgiving let your requests be made known to God" (Phil. 4:6). Such a sense of God's presence, he said, would give them the "peace of God, which passes all understanding" (Phil. 4:7).

Questions for Discussion

1. What is the difference between anxiety and fear?
2. Do you believe that the human sense of finiteness in the face of uncontrollable problems is a basic cause of anxiety? What is Jesus' remedy for such anxiety?
3. Do you think that a sense of guilt normally causes anxiety?
4. Did God create us in such a way that we feel anxious when we live superficially, when we recognize that we are not fulfilling our God-given potential?
5. How important is Jesus' teaching that people who lay up treasure in heaven are freed from much anxiety (Matt. 6:19–21)?
6. What is the two-fold remedy for basic human anxiety prescribed by Jesus (Matt. 6:19–34)?
7. Have you known anxious Christians who were strong Christians? If so, in what ways were they strong?
8. Is it unrealistic to think that mature Christians may, like Frances R. Havergal and John Wesley, reach a place where they have little or no anxiety?

4 The Spirit Creates Life-Building Emotions

The positive emotions provide a favorable psychological-spiritual climate for the Christian. They light up a barren psychic landscape and diminish the debilitating effects of apathy and frustration.

Paul said the positive emotions are important in the Christian life: "For the kingdom of God does not mean food and drink but righteousness and peace and joy in the Holy Spirit" (Rom. 14:17). These emotions are important to both divine and human relationships: ". . . he who thus serves Christ is acceptable to God and approved by men" (Rom. 14:18). Paul is not suggesting that Christians should seek these emotions as ends in themselves. True spirituality is never self-seeking, and mature Christians do not serve Christ for the emotional benefits they may receive. People who do serve God for emotional satisfaction are religious hedonists, or, as John of the Cross described them, "spiritual gluttons."

The positive emotions raise the human potential for meaningful living in two basic ways.

First, they *heighten our perceptions* of persons, objects,

and situations, particularly of the positive traits in other persons and affirmative elements in situations. Positive emotions help us perceive things with more clarity because, with less emotional conflict in our minds, we give "concentrated awareness" to what we look at. Our interior psychic states do much to determine what we see. Only the loving heart sees love in others. Just as the artist sees art forms that others do not and as the musician grasps meanings in music that others miss, so the Christian with positive emotions sees affirmative things in life that others overlook.

Second, positive emotions *strongly motivate* us to seek the positive values. Whatever affects the emotional life of a man affects him most deeply. Most of us are more influenced by emotion than by reason. *Emotion* and *motivation* have a common etymological origin in the Latin word *movere,* which means "to move."

William James said that "cold perceptions," those that are devoid of emotion, have little influence on us. He said, perhaps too strongly, that without emotion we would be totally passive and apathetic: "Conceive yourself, if possible, suddenly stripped of all the emotion with which your world now inspires you, and try to imagine it *as it exists,* purely by itself, without your favorable or unfavorable, hopeful or apprehensive comment. It will be almost impossible for you to realize such a condition of negativity and deadness. No portion of the universe would then have importance beyond another; and the whole collection of its things, and series of its events, would be without significance, character, expression, or perspective."[1]

The positive emotions emphasized most by Paul are love, peace, and joy. Paul considered them essential elements of the Christian life. We shall look at each of these.

Love That Enriches Life

Love is one of the great constructive forces of life, or, as Paul expressed it, "love builds up" (I Cor. 8:1). Jesus made

---

1. *Varieties of Religious Experience* (London: Longmans and Green, 1902), p. 147.

it the central concern of life (Mark 12:29–31). Henry Drummond said it is "the greatest thing in the world." Blanton Smiley said that man must "love or perish." "Analytic therapy," wrote Albert C. Outler, "is essentially an attempt to help the patient gain or regain his capacity for love."[2]

The Holy Spirit broadens and deepens our love by giving us the love of God. ". . . God's love has been poured into our hearts through the Holy Spirit which has been given to us" (Rom. 5:5). Christian love was unknown in the world when Christianity was born. The Greek language, though rich in its vocabulary, had no word big enough to express it. The Greeks had one term for aesthetic love and one for love within the family and between friends, but both were too small to express God's love in the hearts of believers. To solve this problem, the early Christians imbued the word *agapē* with new meanings. The word became "born again," and it and its cognates are used about 250 times in the New Testament.

To understand Christian love we must understand the love of God. God loved sinful man not because man was good and lovable but because the divine nature is one of love. John made this point cogently when he said, "God is love" (I John 4:8). This is one of the great revelations about the character of God, and it is so grand that it is hard for us to grasp. C. H. Dodd said that this single sentence is John's outstanding contribution to theology.

Christian love, which involves the mind as well as the emotions, is made up of three elements: (1) respect and esteem; (2) sentiment and appreciation, or the feelings of love; and (3) mutuality.

Respect for others ennobles life. The Greek word *agapē* has a sturdy rational element in its emphasis upon "respect for" and "esteem of" other persons. It suggests a rational appreciation of what another actually is or of what he may

---

2. *Psychotherapy and the Christian Message* (New York: Harper, 1954), p. 202.

become. It suggests our recognition of the moral worth of persons.

The element of esteem for others is seen in the Christian's love of his enemies, about whom he probably does not feel sentimental. The Christian does have, however, a genuine love of those who have wronged him in that he wishes them well because they too have the dignity of personhood.

When we esteem others, we grow personally. Our interests expand as we spend time with those whose personalities and characters we appreciate. We foster inner strength when we have regard for the personhood of our "enemies" and when we pray for their well-being.

The respect we give to others will be returned. As we appreciate their good qualities, they in turn may respect ours. Thus a climate for growth develops. We are delivered from feelings of anonymity. Moreover, our esteem for others is related to our esteem for ourselves. The recognition of the personhood in others helps us to be thankful for the personhood God gave us.

The sentiments of love deepen life. Genuine sentiments or feelings of love meet some of the deep needs of human personality. They enhance feelings of belongingness and of being needed. They awaken worthy interests within us and motivate us to help those we love. They yield a rich harvest of patience, kindness, goodness, faithfulness, gentleness, and self-control (cf. Gal. 5:22, 23).

We may have "sentiments of love" for things—nature, art, or music, for example—as well as for people, and these sentiments also enrich life. Samuel L. Brengle told of reading "some of the words of Jesus" one morning. Deeply moved, he went for a walk in a Boston park. He reported his feelings: "Oh, how I loved! In that hour I knew Jesus and I loved Him till it seemed that my heart would break with love. I loved the sparrows, I loved the dogs, I loved the horses, I loved the little urchins on the streets, I loved the strangers who hurried past me, I loved the heathen—I loved the whole world."[3]

---

3. *Helps to Holiness* (London: Salvationist, 1955), p. ix.

The sentiments of love enrich us because they dispose us to see lovely things. God wishes us to see "whatever is true, whatever is honorable, whatever is just, whatever is pure, whatever is lovely, whatever is gracious. . . ." (Phil. 4:8). Those who are without love are like the colorblind; they miss much of the beauty that is in the world.

A sense of mutuality broadens life. The sense of mutuality broadens life by establishing many meaningful relationships. Mutuality refers most basically to reciprocal or shared experience. It goes far in delivering us from states of alienation, isolation, and estrangement. No person wishes to be an island.

Loneliness dwarfs and constricts the human spirit; fellowship helps it grow. Our minds and spirits are broadened when we relate to persons of mutual interests and concerns. It has been said that at such times we do more than exchange ideas, we "exchange souls." In mutuality, the ideas of our friends may become our ideas, their insights become truth to us, and their sentiments modify our sentiments. When a great man was asked the secret of his success, he replied, "I had a friend."

The Holy Spirit helps us extend Christian hospitality to all who will receive it. He enables us to discover bases of mutuality in persons who seem estranged from us. He enables us to take the lead in settling disagreements, as Jesus taught us to do, and thus to broaden life by turning adversaries into friends. He enables us to practice brotherhood because the kingdom of God is a great brotherhood.

The element of mutuality in love demands that we be self-giving, that we go beyond the "love of complacency" to the "love of benevolence." The Holy Spirit helps us have some of the attitudes of Calvary—seeking to be actively benevolent, going to great lengths to do good to others.

Peace That Steadies Life

Peace is a highly constructive emotion. Paul found Christian peace so meaningful in his own life that he said it "passes all understanding" (Phil. 4:7). The peace of God enabled him to be content in every circumstance of life (Phil. 4:11).

Peace is one of the basic emotions of the Christian life. At the time of Jesus' birth, the angels announced that Christ had come to give peace to the world (Luke 2:14). Paul said that peace—along with righteousness and joy—is a basic component of the kingdom of God (Rom. 14:17). He also said that it is among the fruit of the Spirit (Gal. 5:22).

Two currents of thought merged to form the basis for the Christian concept of peace: the Greek idea of harmony and the Hebrew idea of personal well-being. Based on these concepts are two others: reconciliation with God and the divine presence in the life of the believer. The Christian does not try to solve his sin problem by the psychological processes of rationalization, denial, and repression, the result of which is like the "foul tranquility" of a stagnant pool. True Christian peace is like a clear pool through which a stream of water runs.

Christian peace does not mean a passive enjoyment free of strife and difficulty. It is not "the imperturbability of the Epicureans, or the apathy of the Stoic, or the contemplation of the mystic."[4] Francois Fenelon, himself something of a mystic, said that "true peace comes not by inaction, but in letting God act through us."[5]

Christian peace is a gift of God's grace. "Grace is the first and the last word of the gospel; and peace—perfect spiritual soundness—is the finished work of grace."[6] Paul opened nearly all of his epistles with the salutation, "grace and peace."

Peace and hostility. The peace of God displaces its antithesis, hostility to God, as we open the doors of our lives to the heavenly Father's love. God "the enemy" be-

---

4. Raymond T. Stamm, "Galatians: Introduction and Exegesis," in *The Interpreter's Bible*, ed. George L. Buttrick, 12 vols. (Nashville: Abingdon-Cokesbury, 1951–1957), 10:567.

5. *Guide to True Peace* (New York: Harper, 1946), p. xi.

6. James Denney, *The Second Epistle to the Corinthians* (London: Hodder and Stoughton, 1894), p. 11.

comes God "our loving Father." Peace with God removes deep tensions in our lives. It does away with guilt and anxiety that made us antagonistic to God. The removal of antagonism is shown clearly in the conversion of a profane sinner, who exchanges his profanity for praise to God.

The inner peace that comes through reconciliation with God affects deeply our relationships with our fellows. Unknowingly, as it were, we bring peace to our personal environments. An inner calmness and tranquility enable us to view interpersonal problems calmly, to see stresses realistically, and to search for creative ways to handle personal differences. A deep sense of indebtedness to God for the remission of our own sins motivates us to forgive others as God pardoned us.

Christian peace is always characterized by harmony. An interior sense of harmony enables us to live harmoniously with others. There is harmony with God in obedience, harmony with others in brotherhood, and harmony with self in sincerity.

Peace and anxiety. Christian peace is an effective therapy for anxiety because it is born in a consciousness of spiritual strength and rooted in a deep personal awareness of God's provision of adequate spiritual resources. Paul was free from anxiety over his thorn in the flesh because God had assured him, "My grace is sufficient for you. . . ." (II Cor. 12:9).

Paul said in Philippians 4:7 that "peace is a sentinel who 'mounts guard' over the hearts and thoughts of believers." This suggests, said Gerald R. Cragg, "the image . . . of a citadel beset by foes without, manned within by a garrison often turbulent and unreliable. In these circumstances it is 'the peace of God' which both subdues the enemy and disciplines the defenders."[7]

Christian peace involves more than the "peace of mind" spoken of by some psychologists, the relative freedom from anxiety that comes about through increased self-understanding and self-acceptance. Christian peace dispels

---

7. "Romans: Exposition," in *The Interpreter's Bible,* 9:452.

anxiety because it is irradiated with the divine presence, because it puts Christians in touch with ultimate reality.

Joy That Strengthens Life

The Holy Spirit enabled the early Christians to be joyful even in difficult times, times of personal discipline, of personal loss, and of suffering. Paul said that Christians should "rejoice . . . always," that is, in every circumstance of life (Phil. 4:4). This is possible because the risen Christ is with us and gives us attitudes of forbearance and "patience under provocation." Paul knew that sorrow and joy might exist together, forming a creative synthesis of life. After listing in II Corinthians some of his own greatest troubles, he said he was "sorrowful, yet always rejoicing" (6:10). "Joy does not displace sorrow," Friedrich Schleiermacher said, "but both overspread one's entire being."

The joy of Christians in difficulty comes not through the denial and rationalization of their difficulties but from the interior presence of the Holy Spirit. The source of a Christian's joy is the Spirit within Him; the evidence of his joy is his confidence that the Spirit will enable him to cope with

every difficulty. The early Christians were strong because the Spirit led them into exhilarating thoughts—that they had been freed from the guilt and burden of their sins, that they had been called to work with God in fulfilling His eternal purposes, that God would give them strength for the life to which He had called them. They, like William Wordsworth, "felt a presence" that disturbed them with the "joy of elevated thoughts." William Lyon Phelps said that the happiest man is the man who has the most interesting thoughts.

The early Christians had a healthy spiritual fortitude because they saw meaning in their suffering. Paul and Silas sang hymns in a wretched dungeon because they knew they were doing the work of Christ (Acts 16:25). Paul wrote his most joyous epistle, Philippians, in a prison as he faced execution. He was happy and confident because of his continuing ministry to Christians and because of his hope of being in heaven with the risen Christ (Phil. 1:12–26). The

Christians to whom the Epistle to the Hebrews was written had taken joyfully the destruction of their possessions because they believed they "possessed something better and more lasting" (Heb. 10:34 NEB).

Moreover, the early Christians were resolute in suffering because they believed it helped to build personal character which has eternal worth. Peter wrote, "In this you rejoice, though now for a little while you may have to suffer various trials, so that the genuineness of your faith, more precious than gold which though perishable is tested by fire, may redound to praise and glory and honor at the revelation of Jesus Christ" (I Peter 1:6, 7). Basil observed similarly, "For, as the toils of the contests lead the athletes on to their crowns, so also the test through tribulations leads Christians on to perfection, if we receive with becoming patience and in all gratitude what is dispensed to us by the Lord."[8] A Christian may remain joyful if he believes, with Francis de Sales, that "God never permits anything to come upon us as a trial or test of our virtue without desiring that we should profit by it."

Conclusion

The Holy Spirit seeks to make Christians emotionally adequate by helping them have positive emotions. These support human life and help us live fully and effectively. Negative emotions, on the other hand, tend to make life burdensome and unproductive. Positive emotions help us remain steady in difficult situations. They give an optimistic tone to life that enables us to live with confidence. They assist in clearing away the mists of guilt and anxiety so that we can clearly perceive worthy objectives and the lasting values of life. They broaden our interests, deepen our sentiments, increase our zest, and give us strength for life. As Nehemiah said, ". . . do not be grieved, for the joy of the Lord is your strength" (Neh. 8:10).

---

8. *Letters*, trans. A. C. Way, 2 vols. (Washington, D.C.: Catholic University of America, 1951), 1:225.

Questions for Discussion

1. Paul named love as the first fruit of the Spirit. Do you think he thought of love as the forerunner of the other fruits? Is love the most important of the positive emotions?
2. Is the love of Christians different from the love of others? If so, how?
3. Sometimes Christians say that they do not have a great deal of love for others. What can they do to increase their love?
4. Is there a difference between the love that a Christian has for his friends and the love that he has for his "enemies"? If so, what is the difference? Can love of enemies be genuine?
5. A celebrated minister preached a great sermon entitled "The Expulsive Power of a New Affection." Does love always displace hostility? Can one be hostile to one whom he loves?
6. What are the basic elements of Christian peace?
7. Does one's inherited temperament determine in part how much peace a Christian may have as an adult?
8. What new elements did the early Christians add to the then-prevailing concept of joy? Is there still a difference between the joy of believers and the joy of unbelievers?
9. Do you think unbelievers regard Christians as a joyful lot? Why?
10. Is there a difference between joy and pleasure?
11. Is it true that one will be happy if one settles well the three basic problems of life: (1) a vocation, (2) a marriage partner, and (3) a religious faith? Why?

Part 2

The Holy Spirit Strengthens Our Devotional Lives

5 **The Spirit** Enables Us to Perceive Truth

Jesus taught that an important part of the Holy Spirit's work is to lead us into truth. "When the Spirit of truth comes, he will guide you into all the truth. . . ." (John 16:13; cf. 14:26; 15:26; 16:7–15). William Barclay called this "one of the most important texts in all Scripture,"[1] and one reason for its importance is that a knowledge of truth is essential to our Christian lives.

Psychology emphasizes that the character of our perceptions does much to determine the character of our lives. To a large extent, we are what we have perceived and what we now perceive. Changes in behavior are the direct result of changes in our perceptual fields.

Our Christian lives are shallow if our perception of spiritual truth is shallow. Our lives are built on error if we perceive spiritual truth erroneously. Our Christian growth depends on our growing perception of truth. The Christians to whom the Epistle to the Hebrews was addressed had

---

1. *The Promise of the Spirit* (Philadelphia: Westminster, 1960), p. 40.

stopped growing because they had become spiritually imperceptive (5:11). They were spiritual infants, retarded because of their lack of spiritual knowledge (5:12–14).

The Holy Spirit enlightens our minds by enabling us to perceive truth in the Bible. He helps us to see Biblical truths that are new to us; He aids us in seeing fuller meaning in familiar truths. The Protestant Reformers saw clearly that the guidance of the Spirit is essential to interpreting the Bible. Martin Luther said that the Bible is a whole sea full of God's Word and that the Spirit must guide us into that truth. John Calvin said, "The word [of God] is . . . like the sun which shines upon all, but is of no use to the blind. . . . hence the word cannot penetrate our mind unless the Spirit, that internal teacher, by his enlightening power make an entrance for it."[2] The Belgic Confession suggests that without the Holy Spirit's aid a man can neither perceive Holy Scripture nor be subject to it.[3]

The Spirit's Concern for Human Perception

The Holy Spirit, as the divine author of God's Word, planned the Bible so that the human race, with His assistance, would be able to perceive divine truth in it. He led the human authors of Scripture to use large portions of material that center in real human experience. The triune God did much more than this, however, to reveal divine truth. The Godhead sent Christ into the world as a man to show to the human race the nature of God. The incarnation of Christ arose out of the Deity's concern both that man might be redeemed and that man might perceive God's love for man. The record of Jesus, as incarnate Lord, is found only in the Bible.

Real human experience in the Bible. The men and women of the Bible are not fictitious characters stepping out on an

---

2. *Institutes of the Christian Religion*, trans. Henry Beveridge (Grand Rapids: Eerdmans, n.d.), 3.2.34.

3. Article 5.

imaginary stage to dramatize life. Neither were they idealists speaking out of a poverty of experience. Rather, they were real persons facing representative problems of life. Sometimes they succeeded; at other times they failed. The youthful Joseph, tempted in Potiphar's house, shows us the worth of personal integrity. David and Jonathan tell us that true friendship is worth more than selfish gain. On the other hand, the temptation of Peter on the night before Jesus' crucifixion helps us perceive the human weakness in which all of us share.

The Holy Spirit led many of the Biblical writers to share some of their deepest experiences with us. The writers, especially of the Psalms, spoke freely of their anxieties and resulting frustrations, of their hostilities and their sense of estrangement from God, of their guilt and their deep desires for forgiveness. They wrote about being depressed and feeling defeated. On the other hand, they told us of the personal victories that came through faith, of their aspirations and their joys. Their lives speak to us even though separated by many centuries. Human emotions have not changed qualitatively.

Christ's incarnation and human perception. God's concern that we perceive divine truth is dramatically apparent in the incarnation. Christ said, ". . . he who has seen me has seen the Father. . . ." (John 14:9). The Son of God became a man and lived among men so that we might perceive the character of God.

The human race has always found it difficult to believe in abstract goodness. Jesus made divine goodness highly perceptible as He ministered in Galilee, casting out devils, healing the sick, and raising the dead. He Himself was without sin (John 8:46) and was "full of grace and truth" (John 1:14). In one place Peter characterized Christ's work as follows: ". . . he went about doing good and healing all that were oppressed by the devil, for God was with him" (Acts 10:38).

The incarnate Christ demonstrated divine love so clearly that all could see it, finally dying on the cross for our sins. The cross of Christ stands as God's assurance of His boundless love of the human race.

New Perceptions Through New Life

The character of the reader largely determines what he sees in the Bible and how he sees it. As we said before, psychology emphasizes that "we see things not as they are but as we are." An ancient philosopher observed, "Eyes and ears are bad witnesses to those who have barbarous souls." Jesus said that the multitudes to whom He spoke were unable to understand His message because their hearts were dull: ". . . seeing they do not see, and hearing they do not hear, nor do they understand" (Matt. 13:13).

This is where the Holy Spirit helps us. He increases our readiness to perceive spiritual truth by creating within us new life, one with an affinity for spiritual truth. This affinity urges us to seek truth and helps us to perceive spiritual reality. We search for truth as a nutrient as surely as physical forms of life seek food.

Personal spiritual renewal is necessary for one to read the Bible with perception because *like* can be understood only by *like.* Knowledge presumes participation. The soul can know little divine truth unless it has divine life within it. The more our souls are conformed to the divine image, the more truth we will grasp from God's Word. Knowledge is often proportional to affiliation.

What some spiritual leaders said. An early supporter of the German Protestant Reformation emphasized that the reader of Scripture, the written Word, must know Christ, the living Word. "If a man is to understand spiritual things and to know and judge rightly, he must bring the divine Light to the Scriptures, the Spirit to the letter, the Truth to the picture, and the Master to his created work. . . . In a word, to understand the Scriptures a man must become a new man; he must be in Christ who gave forth the Scriptures."[4] Another German Reformer, Sebastian Franck, said: "He who wishes to know what is in the temple [of truth] must not stand outside, merely hearing people read

4. In Rufus Jones, *Spiritual Reformers in the Sixteenth and Seventeenth Centuries* (Boston: Beacon, 1959), p. 74.

and talk about God. . . . He must go inside and have the experience himself."

Calvin wrote that "the soul, when illumined by him [the Spirit of God], receives as it were a new eye, enabling it to contemplate heavenly mysteries, by the splendour of which it was previously dazzled. And thus, indeed, it is only when the human intellect is irradiated by the light of the Holy Spirit that it begins to have a taste of those things which pertain to the kingdom of God; previously it was too stupid and senseless to have any relish for them."[5]

John Wesley said that the natural man "has scarce any knowledge of the invisible world, as he has scarce any intercourse with it. Not that it is afar off: no, he is in the midst of it; it encompasses him round about. . . . But when he is born of God, born of the Spirit, how is the matter of his existence changed! His whole soul is now sensible of God. . . ."[6]

How the Spirit increases spiritual perception. The Holy Spirit increases our readiness to perceive truth in God's Word by increasing our *sense of need of spiritual truth.* Our attention and perceptions are greatly conditioned by our sense of need. The hungry man is attentive to food; the lonely man wants to relate to people; and the music lover seeks out the music he enjoys. The eternal spirit in us, thirsting for reality, is questing for truth because that is its most basic need. As a tireless philosopher seeks eagerly for truth, so the immortal spirit within us tries to perceive what is in the Word of God. It says, "Light, more light."

The Holy Spirit helps us have the *courage to receive deep and radical truths* that criticize us. He helps us avoid escape and defense mechanisms against these truths. There are times when, reading the Word, we may say with the disciples, "This is a hard saying, who can listen to it?" (John 6:60). But if we reject God's truth, we shall settle down at a half-way house of truth. If we accept God's truth, we shall go on to fuller life. Soren Kierkegaard said that one of the greatest faults of man is the wish to hear half-truths.

---

5. *Institutes* 3.2.34.
6. *Works,* 14 vols. (Grand Rapids: Zondervan, 1958–1959), 5:226.

The Holy Spirit enhances our perception of spiritual truth by bringing about *deep changes in our thought life.* He expands the borders of our provincial ideas to include the realm of the Spirit. He shows us that the truths on which we base our lives are ultimately spiritual and not physical, that only the knowledge of spiritual realities will have worth in the beyond.

The Holy Spirit increases our spiritual perception by enhancing our *transcendental interests.* We see our lives as a continuum extending into the eternal ages, and this gives us a great sense of stewardship. We see clearly that spiritual values are basic, that they alone will abide forever. This concern about our lives, both for the now and for the beyond, causes us to seek God's truth in the Bible.

Johannes Scotus Erigena prayed fittingly: "O Lord Jesus, I ask no other reward, no other blessing, no other joy, than to understand in a pure manner, without error due to false speculation, thy words inspired by the Holy Spirit. There indeed lies the summit of happiness, the goal of perfect contemplation. Beyond that, even the most pure among rational souls will find nothing, since nothing is beyond. . . ."[7]

Avoiding Selective Perceptions

Some of us have attitudes that cause us to be selective when we read the Bible. We have unconscious dispositions to perceive only the truths that we want to perceive. These dispositions cause us to see some truths immediately and clearly and other truths with great difficulty or not at all. They create in us a defense against truths that are disagreeable to us or that are beyond the range of our interests.

Some of us have become particularly fond of some Biblical truths we have known from childhood, which may hinder us in the discovery of new truths. Having become nostalgic about certain parts of the Bible, we may neglect other parts. Satisfaction with a little knowledge of the Bible

---

7. In James Walsh, *Spirituality Through the Centuries* (New York: Kenedy, 1964), p. 89.

may prevent us from obtaining a fuller knowledge. We become mountain climbers who stop short of the summit at a pleasant spot, unaware that at the summit is a far more exhilarating view.

Familiarity sometimes diminishes our readiness to see new truths in the Bible. Rereading the Bible is sometimes like traveling on a road that we have taken before: the expectancy and anticipation that we had the first time are gone. Thus, when we read great concepts in the Bible, we are unmoved by them. When we read about great men, we are not impressed. When we read about miraculous events, we fail to recognize the hand of God in them.

Our prejudices, much like our traditions, may cause us to be selective in what we see in the Bible. They put some passages in large type and others in small print, and we usually read the small print casually or not at all.

The Holy Spirit helps diminish our selectivity. He broadens our view of truth. He shows us that the truth of the Bible is far greater than any human formulation of it. He makes dynamic the Biblical truth that is familiar to us, and we are then motivated to seek more truth. He surely permits us to appreciate those elements of our Christian traditions that are based on Biblical truth, but He also helps us, as He did John Robinson, to feel deeply that "the Lord has more truth yet to break forth out of his holy Word." He reveals to us that the Bible is a great continent of truth of which we have explored only a very small part.

Victory over a Dull Spiritual Mood

One of the greatest obstacles to perceiving truth in the Bible is a dull spiritual mood. The term *mood* itself refers to certain rational-emotional dispositions that affect our mental perceptivity. Spiritual mood refers to the dispositions of the soul or the human spirit. A dull Christian mood is one of spiritual apathy and inertia, of diminished aspirations and enthusiasm.

Secularized education has disposed some of us to dull spiritual moods. It trained us only to see physical things, earthly realities, and temporal values; excessive attention to these things causes dull spiritual moods. Jesus said that perception of spiritual truth is destroyed "by the cares and riches and pleasures of life" (Luke 8:14; cf. Luke 21:34). The cares and earthly pleasures of life can make us weary, and when we come to the Word of God physically and emotionally weary, we are ill prepared to see God's truth in His Word. Excessive attention to earthly things also can produce anxiety, and this too hinders our perception of truth. It clouds our view of eternal values as do dirty eyeglasses. The problem of earthly distraction is greater today than it has been before because so many interests call for our attention. All of us are surrounded by many enticing worldly stimuli. "We are distracted from distraction by distraction."

Dullness in spiritual perception comes also when we are hesitant to do God's will. Like schoolchildren who fail to hear the things they do not wish to hear, we sometimes are slow to understand a difficult assignment. Many of the people who heard Jesus speak in Galilee did not understand what He said because they had no desire to do the will of God. Their hearts had become gross and unperceiving. When we are unwilling to do God's will, our minds, quite unknown to us, put a sentry at the doors of our understanding and the sentry closes the door to all disturbing thoughts. As a perceptual vigilante, it protects our egos. The Holy Spirit, on the other hand, helps us see that God's will for us is not arbitrary but benevolent, and this readies our hearts to accept His will.

Bonaventura said that when our minds are spiritually dull, we "read [the Bible] without unction, speculate without devotion, investigate without wonder, examine without exultation, work without piety, know without love, understand without humility, . . . [are] zealous without divine grace, see without wisdom divinely inspired."[8] The Bible is dull when we are dull. A worldly spirit shuts the Bible and hides its truths from us. But when we are committed to do God's will, the Bible comes alive. In such times the "East

---

8. *The Mind's Road to God,* trans. George Boas (Indianapolis: Bobbs-Merrill, 1953), p. 5.

windows of divine surprise" within us open, and we see truth that is new to us.

Conclusion

The Holy Spirit uses many means to prepare our minds to perceive the truth of the Bible. He makes us quest for truth. He gives us open attitudes toward the truth He wishes us to see. He helps us lay aside prejudices—our grasp of half-truths—so that we may perceive the full truth. He frees our minds of anxieties and makes us quiet and alert. He increases our spiritual sensitivity. He strengthens our intuitive powers. He awakens memories of truths which prepare our minds to perceive deeper truths.

Questions for Discussion

1. On the night before Jesus was crucified, He said more about the Holy Spirit than He had before. For His specific words, see John 14:16–18, 26; 15:26; 16:7–15. How prominent in these references is the idea that the Holy Spirit is the revealer of truth?
2. What was the central point of Jesus' teaching on spiritual perception in Matthew 13:1–17?
3. Do you think that our perceptions are affected deeply by our inner character? In what sense do we see things "as *we* are and not as *things* are"?
4. How does anxiety affect our perceptions?
5. How does hostility affect our perceptions?
6. What have you done to overcome a dull spiritual attitude while reading the Bible?
7. Have you found that familiarity with some portion of the Bible has hindered you from seeing deeper truths in it? If so, what did you do to overcome that handicap?
8. Does familiarity with the Scriptures provide also a basis for the discovery of deeper truths?
9. Are there genuine values in the appreciation of our Christian and denominational traditions? If so, what are some of these values? What are some dangers of appreciating our traditions too exclusively?

6 The Spirit Helps Us Read the Bible

Bernard of Clairvaux was deeply moved by the thought that the Scriptures are God's "meeting place" with man. He believed that "God had enshrined himself" in the sacred Scriptures so that those who read the Word might perceive His character. The Scriptures are a place of divine-human encounter; the Holy Spirit meets openhearted readers there and helps them perceive divine truth.

The Illuminated Word

The divine revealer becomes the divine illuminator to all of those who read the Bible in faith. "The Spirit of God not only once inspired those who wrote it [the Bible]," John Wesley said, "but continually inspires, supernaturally assists, all that read it with earnest prayer."[1] More than four

---

1. *Explanatory Notes on the New Testament* (New York: Mason and Lane, 1839), p. 554. Compare with this comment on II Timothy 3:16, Wesley's comments on Acts 7:38, John 15:3, and Hebrews 4:12.

hundred years ago, Dirck Coornhart, a Reformer in Holland, said that the Bible is a lantern through which the light of the Spirit shines. Both the Bible as the lantern and the Holy Spirit as the light within it are necessary to those who seek to know spiritual truth. All of us, regardless of our situations, are, when we read the Bible, like men sitting in the dim twilight. We all need to let light from the Spirit fall on its pages.

The character of the Spirit's illumination. We should not think of the divine illumination of Scripture as something enigmatic and unrealistic. Illumination is simply the Holy Spirit's work of guiding Christians into all truth (John 16:13). *Inspiration* means "inbreathing," and it is a cognate of the word *spirit.* God continues to breathe upon the human spirit through the ministry of the Holy Spirit.

In His work of enlightenment, the Holy Spirit shares the divine consciousness with us (I Cor. 2:12–16). In a real sense some of God's perspective becomes our perspective, and some of God's thoughts become our thoughts. The Holy Spirit gives us "the mind of Christ," increasing our ability to see things as Christ saw them. The Spirit does not, as William Temple explained, hand down intellectual propositions about God, but He creates a relationship between us and God that helps us see the truths of God.

The divine illumination assists all Christians to perceive and interpret the truth recorded in the Bible. The divine presence is a creative addition to our natural capacities. Thomas a Kempis portrayed the Spirit as saying: "Await my coming and my heavenly visitation and bear patiently the exile and dryness of your heart until you shall be visited by me, and delivered by me from all tediousness and disquiet of mind. When I come, I shall make you forget all your former labors and you will have inward rest and quiet of soul. I shall also lay open before you the flourishing meadow of Holy Scripture, and with great gladness of heart you will know the truest understanding of it."[2]

---

2. *Imitation of Christ,* ed. Harold C. Gardiner, trans. Richard Whitford (Garden City, N.Y.: Doubleday, 1955), p. 182.

The Spirit's illumination in history. The Holy Spirit demonstrated His ministry of unfolding divine truth when on the day of Pentecost He disclosed to the disciples new and deeper meanings of the Old Testament Scriptures. Peter, speaking for the group, declared new and revolutionary insights from the Hebrew Scriptures, by the inspiration of the Spirit: the coming of the Holy Spirit on that day fulfilled the prophecy of Joel (Acts 2:16–21); Christ's resurrection fulfilled the words of David (Acts 2:24–28); Christ's exaltation into heaven and His ultimate triumph over sin are envisioned in the Old Testament (Acts 2:32–35).

The Holy Spirit had the crucial task after Pentecost of revealing to the disciples the ultimate nature of the kingdom of God. Until Pentecost the disciples believed that the kingdom was to be an earthly establishment of Jewish people; after Pentecost the apostles saw first that God's kingdom was spiritual (Rom. 14:17), and then that it was not to be made up only of Jewish people. The Spirit helped Peter see that "God shows no partiality, but in every nation any one who fears him and does what is right is acceptable to him" (Acts 10:34, 35). Later Paul perceived that all persons may be saved by faith (Rom. 1:17; 5:1).

The Holy Spirit's ministry of illuminating Scriptural truth continues to this present day, and a comprehensive survey of this ministry would be very lengthy indeed. One more dramatic period in history when His work was extensive and deep was the Reformation, when the Protestants rediscovered forgotten truths of the Bible and the Bible was restored to its central place in the lives of the people.

The Spirit's illumination today. The Holy Spirit helps us see the deeper truths of the Biblical words we read. Many of us have become accustomed to perceive only that which meets the eye in our reading of newspapers and current books, and we do not look beyond the words themselves for deeper meanings. We are like the twelve disciples who were disposed to look only at the obvious and immediate meanings of Jesus' words (Matt. 16:1–12; Acts 1:6, 7). Reading in depth is especially important when we read the Bible because the revelation of divine truth sometimes goes beyond the immediate meaning of words.

Human reason is limited in grasping the deep truths of the Bible without the help of the Spirit. The writer of that medieval treatise *The Mirror of Simple Souls* said, "O understanding of reason! what thou hast of rudeness! Thou takest of the shell of the chaff and leavest the kernel of the grain."[3]

The help of the Holy Spirit in reading the Bible has great practical value to us, helping us live victorious Christian lives, see ourselves as God sees us, and see God's grace and power to help us. He leads us to Biblical truth that provides nutrients to our souls, to verses that provide strength in hours of temptation and courage in times of fear. He helps us build our theological convictions out of many Biblical materials, as a craftsman uses many pieces of material to construct a house. For instance, we take many Biblical materials about the deity of our Lord and synthesize them. In doing this, we follow the method of Jesus' twelve disciples. After Jesus spoke divine truth to them and worked miracles before them, they finally confessed with deep inner conviction, "Thou art the Christ, the Son of the living God" (Matt. 16:16 KJV).

The Enlivened Word

The Holy Spirit causes the Bible to come alive to those who are alive in Christ. The Epistle to the Hebrews says that "the word of God is alive and active. . . . It sifts the purposes and thoughts of the heart" (Heb. 4:12 NEB). Paul said of the written law of God that the letter kills but the Spirit gives life (II Cor. 3:6). Written codes have no power per se to motivate one to the spiritual life, but the Spirit gives the Bible that power. Thomas a Kempis said that reading the Bible without the presence of the Spirit "can perfect me little." Thomas acknowledged to God that the books of the Bible "speak your words, but they do not give the spirit to understand the words. They speak fair, but if you are

3. In Evelyn Underhill, *The Essentials of Mysticism* (London: Dent, 1920), p. 149.

silent, they do not kindle the heart. They show forth your letters, but you interpret the sentence. They reveal great high mysteries, but you open the true understanding of them. They declare your commandments, but you help to their performance. They show the way but you give strength to walk in it. They do all outwardly, but you illuminate and instruct the heart within. They water externally, but you give the inward growth."[4]

Walter Hilton, a fourteenth-century student of Christian spirituality, asserted that a knowledge of Biblical facts and literature can be acquired by any intelligent person. Indeed, "oftentimes heretics, hypocrites, and fleshly-living men have more such knowledge than true Christian men."[5] But this knowledge is "only [a] similitude and shadow" of the knowledge that the Spirit will give. Apart from the Spirit's presence, the Word "lacks the spiritual savoring of God and the inner sweetness of love."[6] But if those who have a merely human knowledge of the Bible "will offer it in humility to our Lord and ask his favor he will turn the water into wine as he did by his blessing in response to his mother at the marriage feast. In other words, he will turn this tasteless knowledge into wisdom, the cold and naked reason into spiritual light and burning love by the gift of the Holy Spirit."[7]

The Holy Spirit also helps us obey the Biblical words that He reveals to us. Thomas admitted to God that without the Spirit's help, he would "die and be made like a man without fruit, warmed from without, but not inflamed within; and so receive the harder judgment because I have heard your word and not done it, known it and not loved it, believed it and not fulfilled it."[8]

---

4. *Imitation of Christ* (Philadelphia: Altemus, 1894), p. 104.

5. *The Scale of Perfection,* ed. Walter Hilton (London: Watkins, 1923), p. 7.

6. Ibid., p. 6.

7. Ibid., p. 8.

8. *Imitation of Christ* (Philadelphia: Altemus, 1894), p. 105.

The Internalized Word

Jeremiah looked forward to the dispensation of the Holy Spirit when, in God's words, "I will put my law within them, and I will write it upon their hearts; and I will be their God, and they shall be my people" (Jer. 31:33). This verse is a mountain peak of Old Testament revelation.

Paul told the Corinthians that the Spirit had written the truth of Christ upon their hearts: ". . . you show that you are a letter from Christ delivered by us, written not with ink but with the Spirit of the living God, not on tablets of stone but on tablets of human hearts" (II Cor. 3:3). He exhorted the Colossians to "let the word of Christ dwell in you richly, as you teach and admonish one another in all wisdom, and as you sing psalms and hymns and spiritual songs with thankfulness in your hearts to God" (Col. 3:16).

The process of internalization. The Spirit of truth helps all of us as Christians to internalize revealed Scriptural truth. He enables us to incorporate it into our lives so that it becomes a part of our inmost selves, to assimilate it into our thinking so that it begins to motivate us.

How does the Holy Spirit internalize Biblical truth? He does it in large part by motivating us to do it ourselves. He gives us a love of the Bible and a strong desire to identify with spiritual truth. He leads us to see deep meanings in the Bible. Sometimes He makes passages that are particularly relevant to us stand out with an unusual glow and vigor. He leads us to say with Peter, "Lord, to whom shall we go? You have the words of eternal life" (John 6:68).

The Holy Spirit helps us internalize many kinds of Biblical materials. He helps us identify with the spiritual aspirations of Biblical characters, with their undying loyalty to Christ, and with their self-giving attitudes. He enables us to incorporate the Bible's teaching that the spiritual life is all-important, that a man who gains the whole world and loses his own soul profits nothing.

Internalization and the prayer life. The Holy Spirit strengthens our prayer lives by internalizing in us, for instance, Isaiah's view of the majesty of God. This is important because genuine prayer always takes place in the atmosphere of divine reverence. We become thankful to God when we deeply perceive His manifold goodness to us as portrayed in the Bible. Our ability to praise our heavenly Father increases as we assimilate the words of praise in, for instance, the Psalms.

Moreover, the Spirit helps us assimilate the conviction of Biblical men and women that prayer is one of the necessities of life. We come to feel that the relevance of prayer is as broad as human need, for persons in the Scriptures prayed for both great and small things, for both temporal and spiritual blessings. Moreover, as we deeply perceive Jesus' words about our heavenly Father's concern for us, we find ourselves ready to pray about every need in life.

The Holy Spirit convinces us of God's unflagging concern for men as we read in both the Old and New Testaments about His helpfulness to them, and so we trust God to answer our prayers. We take relevant promises of God and make them our own. The miracles of Christ assure us that our risen Lord will help us. We internalize the belief that He is the same yesterday and today and forever (Heb. 13:8).

Internalization and Christian conduct. The Holy Spirit strengthens our dispositions to live righteously as we internalize Biblical teachings on the godly life. New motives for Christian conduct come into existence; new ethical interests are born; new moral objectives come into view; new attitudes arise; and a new moral sensitivity pervades our inner lives. Moral ambivalence decreases, and an ethical spontaneity arises. Our motives to do right come increasingly from within and not from some exterior source such as a moral code book.

When we interiorize the Biblical objectives for human life, we go gladly in the direction in which these guideposts point. We avoid the hesitancy that often comes from following exterior commands. These interiorized Biblical objectives provide a good basis for the "better self" to reprove and correct the "wayward self." We are ready to accept self-reproof for we have identified with the truth on which the reproof is founded. We do not feel like servants following exterior commands, but like sons doing the father's will—which has become our will.

Furthermore, the Holy Spirit interiorizes with us many doctrinal teachings that motivate us to live Christian lives. Our belief in God's love motivates us to love Him. Our belief in God's power motivates us to live victorious lives, constantly drawing on that power. Our belief that God forgives, motivates us to avoid sin. Our belief in divine guidance motivates us to seek God's guidance for our lives.

Internalization and Christian growth. Some psychologists believe that a child's identification with the ideas and the morals of his parents is the most important principle in the child's growth, and the Christian's internalization of spiritual truth is just as important in his Christian growth.

A person may never identify with moral principles and still be moral, but he does not have a good character because character is always based on inwardness. A person may be ethical because he fears punishment, or because he wishes the approval of good people, or because of some other reason. One cannot, however, be a genuine Christian without internalizing spiritual truth. Inwardness is a distinctive and basic element in the Christian religion. This was one of Jesus' primary emphases (see, for example, Matt. 5–7), and it stood in sharp contrast to the teachings of other religious leaders of His day.

Conclusion

The Bible is the great textbook of life. It provides divine wisdom for persons who seek to live fulfilled lives. It was given by God so "that the man of God may be complete, equipped for every good work" (II Tim. 3:17). It is "profitable for teaching, for reproof, for correction, and for training in righteousness" (II Tim. 3:16).

The Spirit is our tutor when we, as Christians, read the textbook of life. He creates within us a strong desire for God's truth and enables us to receive this truth. He quiets our earthly anxieties so that we may give attention to the Word. He gives us a spiritual-mindedness that enables us to understand divine truth. Paul said that Christians understand spiritual things because "we have the mind of Christ" (I Cor. 2:14–16). Much of Christian truth must be practiced to be known, and the Holy Spirit helps us to respond to the truth we know; each response helps prepare the way for fuller knowledge of the Word.

Questions for Discussion

1. The Protestant Reformers emphasized the need of the Spirit's help in interpreting the Bible. How important is this principle?
2. Can we know the specific times that the Spirit guides us in interpreting the message of the Bible? If so, how?
3. Is there a real danger that we, as sincere Christians, may think that our own impressions of and thoughts about Biblical truth come from the Spirit when in reality they come from our own minds?
4. How do you account for the fact that sincere Christians often differ on basic interpretations of Biblical truth?
5. Do you believe that the primary way of knowing God is through Bible reading that is guided by the Spirit?
6. Do you think that the Holy Spirit reveals truth to Christians through anything other than the Bible? If so, what?
7. To what extent can unbelievers understand the Bible?
8. List some of the ways in which the Spirit prepares Christians to read the Bible.
9. How important is it for Christians to internalize Biblical truth?
10. Name some of the human conditions that are favorable to the internalization of Biblical truth.
11. Name some ways in which the Bible is the textbook of life.

7 The Spirit Gives Us a Mood to Pray

The Holy Spirit prepares us for prayer by creating within us a mood of spiritual fervency and a sense of our need for God. Moreover, His presence in our lives makes real to us the spiritual values, creating within us a deep desire for the things that are eternal. He imparts to us a spiritual concern that motivates us to pray, a confidence that it is one of life's most meaningful activities, and an ability to trust God for answers.

The Spirit helps us overcome spiritual apathy when we pray and moves us from secular attitudes to spiritual ones. Spiritual apathy and a preoccupation with things are the two greatest hindrances to prayer in our times. These are so firmly based within many of us that we must have the help of the Spirit of God to overcome them. The Spirit also helps us have a positive mood for prayer as we engage in Christian meditation and praise to God.

Overcoming Spiritual Apathy

The word *apathy* is related to the Latin term *acedia*, which suggests a "don't care" attitude, and it has been defined as "carelessness." It is a kind of emotional passivity that fills an unperceptive and sluggish mind. Apathy in prayer is human tedium and torpor in the divine presence.

Every Christian at times has a problem of apathy in his prayer life, for this tendency to indolence is deeply rooted in man's psychophysical nature. Psychologist M. Esther Harding considered sloth "the most fundamental and deep-seated urge in the psyche."[1] Some medieval theologians considered sloth one of seven cardinal sins. It was one of the basic problems of those to whom the Epistle to the Hebrews was addressed. These Christians, having grown indolent, had become fixated at the early levels of the Christian life. The writer urged them to overcome their apathy and to reclaim some of the spiritual vigor they had known at the beginning of their Christian lives: ". . . we desire each one of you to show the same earnestness [that you had felt before] in realizing the full assurance of hope until the end, so that you may not be sluggish. . . ." (Heb. 6:11, 12).

John Donne, a man of great religious devotion, found that even small things hindered him in prayer when he was apathetic: "A memory of yesterday's pleasures, a fear of tomorrow's dangers, a straw under my knee, a noise in my ear, a light in my life, an anything, a nothing, a fancy, a chimera in my brain troubles me in my prayers."

We are unperceptive of our spiritual needs when apathetic, and thus we feel little need to pray. John Bunyan portrayed this truth with great clarity in *The Pilgrim's Progress.* Christian found three persons fast asleep at the bottom of a hill. "The name of one was Simple, another Sloth, and the third, Presumption." Christian awakened them and warned that if a roaring lion came by, "you will certainly become a prey to his teeth." The drowsy and apathetic fellows were unimpressed. Simple said, "I see no

---

1. *Journey into Self* (New York: Longmans and Green, 1956), p. 283.

danger." Sloth said, "Yet a little more sleep." Presumption, assuming that he was adequate for his problems, said, "Every tub must stand on its own bottom."

Spiritual apathy makes our prayers shallow and superficial. Having little sense of need and feeling quite adequate, we feel little urge to pray. Apathy makes the will of God seem so arduous that we hesitate to follow it. Our gratitude to God becomes minimal, our affections languid, our desires spiritless, and our hearts cold.

Many Christians find that there are no easy human remedies for apathy in prayer. Increased human effort often fails. One man said frankly that the only way he could get rid of apathy in prayer was to get himself into deep trouble. Then, he said, he could pray with ardor. This statement is revealing, but the method it suggests is unsatisfactory.

Turning away from Secular Attitudes

In addition to the constitutional and perennial problem of apathy, our secular age has created a climate that is unfavorable to prayer. Having been conditioned to feel that personal achievements and earthly success are the basic ends of life, we devote too many of our prayers to begging God to help us in our earthly affairs. We become like beggars who go too frequently to the house of a generous family for handouts without offering anything in return. This makes us feel cheap and exploitative. We have little genuine fellowship with God when our prayers are primarily utilitarian and egocentric. Our overconcern for earthly things fills our minds with worldly ambitions, plans, frustrations, and anxieties, making them unprepared for communion with God. Augustine said that prayers that are largely for earthly things are "carnal prayers."

We must put the highest priority on spiritual things if we are to pray effectively. In prayer, as in all of the Christian life, we must "seek . . . first the kingdom of God and his righteousness" (KJV). Having made spiritual values our primary concern, we pray with an inner certitude that we are engaging in life's most important activity. Such a certitude overcomes utilitarian attitudes in prayer.

We shall observe two basic and constructive ways in which the Holy Spirit assists us to become fervent in prayer. He helps us to meditate on God and on Biblical truth, and He enables us to recognize God's blessings on us. Both of these help to create a good interior climate for prayer.

Giving Attention to Christian Meditation

The Bible commends religious meditation. Paul said to the Christians at Colossae, "Set your minds on things that are above, not on things that are on earth" (Col. 3:2). The psalmist portrayed the spiritually effective person as one who delights in and meditates on God's truth. The first Psalm pictures such a person as "a tree planted by the streams of water, that yields its fruit in its season, and its leaf does not wither. . . ." (Ps. 1:3).

Christian meditation is the act of looking attentively at God and at Christian truth. In meditation we do not undertake to discover new truth but to reflect upon and delight in the truth that we have already grasped. Its primary purpose is to awaken our spiritual faculties so that they may commune with God. Meditation involves several psychic elements, including mental and emotional relaxation, memory, reflection, aspiration, and openness.

Meditation is characterized by interior quietude and expectant listening, which make us aware of God's presence and able to receive divinely given insights. We often discover in meditation that the Spirit has not been absent from us in our busy lives but that we have been too occupied to sense His presence; He has spoken to us, but we have not heard Him.

God communicates with us in meditation, wrote Francois Fenelon, "in a manner which is as insensible to the natural eyes as the falling of dew; but not less refreshing in its secret powers than the dew is to the vegetation."[2]

---

2. Francois Fenelon et al., *A Guide to True Peace,* ed. Howard Brinton (New York: Harper, 1946), p. 12.

Meditation may be difficult. Christian meditation is difficult today because our lives are so full of earthly activities. Many of us find it hard to be alone or quiet. Our situation is different from that of many in earlier generations who, like farmers and craftsmen, worked alone rather than on an assembly line or in a crowded office. Moreover, the mass media have distracted us in our free time by a wide range of enticing programming. As T. S. Eliot said in "Four Quartets," we are

> *Distracted from distraction by distraction*
> *Filled with fancies and empty of meaning*
> *Tumid with apathy with no concentration.*

Meditation on spiritual things is difficult for people who were brought up in highly activistic societies like ours. We have been trained to deal with physical things in our environment, to rely heavily upon the physical senses for the stimuli of thought and action. Most of us are unprepared to meditate, even for a short time, on spiritual things; we must have the help of the Spirit of God.

For many of us, a meditative reading of the Psalms or the Gospels is the best way to begin the practice of meditation. Such reading of the Bible involves both reading and reflecting, stopping again and again in a chapter to think deeply on what we have read and to let the Spirit of God speak to us.

The experiences and needs of the men and women of the Bible are representative of ours, and this makes their words "quick and powerful" to people today. We may be deeply moved when we read about Isaiah's vision of a holy and majestic God (Isa. 6). Again, as we identify with the twelve disciples, we feel that Jesus' words to them are His words to us. Moreover, the Spirit of God helps us sense that Christ is alive and that the ever-living Christ spoke ever-living words. Such experiences prepare us for effective prayer by the help of God's Spirit.

Meditation both disturbs and inspires us. The Holy Spirit helps us perceive ourselves more fully when we reflect upon Biblical truth. He causes God's Word to disturb our spiritual complacency. We see ourselves somewhat from God's perspective as we think of God and His holiness. We do not boast of *our* righteousness when we think of *His* righteousness. We are much aware of our creaturely weakness when we meditate upon our Creator.

The Spirit makes us unwilling to fixate at low spiritual levels. He enables us to aspire to be stronger and more effective Christians. As we meditate on divine truth, we perceive deep needs within us; we see new possibilities for the Christian life; and we become aware of the power of God's grace to help us.

In Christian meditation the mind, led by the memory, turns from earthly concerns to the mental storehouse of spiritual knowledge. Spiritual values appear to have increased worth when looked at in their own setting, away from the foibles and distractions of the world. Warmth and praise steal into the meditative mind as it thinks about God and His eternal goodness. Holy aspirations spring up, and hope certifies that these can be realized through divine grace. Meditation on Christian truth tends to free us from preoccupation with earthly things by creating within us a sense of the reality of the things of God, of their supreme importance in our lives. The Holy Spirit quiets our minds and diminishes our anxiety about earthly matters. Then the eternal spirit within us reaches out for the eternal values. Catherine of Siena said that the heart of the contemplative Christian is emptied of "a disordinate love of transitory things" and "filled with the love of celestial things."

Meditation upon God's truth brings about a healthful fascination for things that are eternal. John Masefield had this kind of fascination, often feeling the presence of a larger life about him, one with "incredible perfection, . . . a brightness not of this world." He believed that life in God is "the source of all that is of glory or goodness in this world; and that modern man, not knowing that life, is dwelling in death."[3]

Augustine, commenting on one of the Psalms, said that the psalmist was drawn to the temple when, "as if from the

---

3. In Anne Fremantle, ed., *The Protestant Mystics* (Boston: Little and Brown, 1964), p. 314.

house of God some instrument was sweetly sounding; and he while walking in the temple, hearing a certain inward sound, led on by its sweetness, and following the guidance of the sound, withdrawing himself from all clamour of flesh and blood, made his way even to the house of God." Augustine added, "There sounds in the ears of the heart a strain; mysterious, melodious and sweet." In meditation we are quiet enough to hear these "sounds" and are drawn to prayer.

There is a direct relationship between our spiritual aspirations and our fervor in prayer. Spiritual emptiness leads to apathetic prayers; spiritual fullness dispels apathy. The quality of our prayers depends heavily on what we want in life. A preponderance of earthly concerns blights the spirit of prayer; a healthful fascination for spiritual things invigorates it.

Recognizing God's Gifts in Thankfulness

A grateful heart is a prerequisite for effective prayer; ungrateful people have little communion with God. Paul urged the Philippians, "In everything by prayer and supplication with thanksgiving let your requests be made known to God" (Phil. 4:6).

Men were created to be in relationship with God, from whom they receive many blessings. They must recognize these blessings as being from God and be thankful for them. When they fail to do so, their relationship with God becomes increasingly estranged. Paul spoke of godless Gentiles who knew God but "glorified him not as God, neither were thankful"; they "became vain in their imaginations, and their foolish heart was darkened" (Rom. 1:21 KJV).

Sincere praise strengthens our sense of fellowship with God and reinforces our feelings of dependence on Him. It helps to free us from the false sense of self-confidence which the secular spirit fosters. The recognition of God's blessings in our lives is a good antidote to feelings of human self-sufficiency, feelings which destroy our need of prayer. Friedrich Schleiermacher believed that the sense of need is the basic motive for prayer—indeed for all religious behavior.

Praise to our heavenly Father for His goodness to us reinforces our sense of his concern for us, which in turn strengthens our disposition to pray.

Praise kindles faith in God. It helps us expect new blessings from our heavenly Father. "He who bears most in mind what has been given him by God will be most emboldened to ask for fresh gifts from above." The nine lepers who did not thank Jesus for healing them disqualified themselves from asking for future blessings. Their ingratitude made them feel unworthy and inhibited them from making further contacts with their benefactor.

Praise to God increases our comprehension of the sufficiency of God's grace. This helps us to be grace-conscious instead of problem-conscious. Our problems look small when viewed against the background of God's sufficiency. When Paul looked at the grace of Christ, he could say, "I can do all things in him who strengthens me" (Phil. 4:13).

Conclusion

Sometimes the Holy Spirit puts Christians in a mood of prayer by giving them an unusual sense of His presence. The Spirit may do this in corporate worship, private devotions, or any other circumstance of life. Bernard of Clairvaux described this experience: "He has awakened my sleeping soul. He has stirred and softened and wounded my heart which was torpid and as hard as a rock. He has started to pluck up and to destroy, to plant and to build, to water areas that were arid and dry, to cast light into areas that were dark with shadow, to throw open those that were shut, to warm with his flame those that were cold . . . so that my soul might bless the Lord and all that is within me might praise his Holy Name. . . ."[4]

More frequently, the Holy Spirit grants us His abiding presence as a continuing preparation for effective prayer. His life in us warms our hearts and enlivens our Christian

---

4. *On the Song of Songs,* ed. and trans. by a religious of C.S.M.V. (London: Mowbray, 1952), p. 230.

aspirations. His holy presence makes us aware of our spiritual needs, and we pray to grow in grace. He makes us sensitive to the suffering of people about us and motivates us to pray for them. He leads us to serve in our churches and elsewhere, and to pray for divine help. We pray for the kingdom of God because we are involved in the work of the kingdom.

Questions for Discussion

1. How important is "mood" in private prayer? In corporate prayer?
2. Some theologians have considered the following sins deadly to the spiritual life: pride, covetousness, lust, anger, gluttony, envy, and sloth. Are these seven capital sins the most harmful? Is sloth, or spiritual apathy, as destructive as the others?
3. In what areas of the Christian life other than prayer is spiritual apathy especially harmful?
4. To what extent was Jesus concerned about secular attitudes among His hearers? See Matt. 13:22; 16:26; 24:38, 39; Luke 21:34.
5. Do you think that things-mindedness is a greater problem among believers today than it was in Jesus' time? In the period of your grandfathers?
6. Some Christians who are rather mystical believe that meditation on spiritual things is a basic element of spiritual growth. Do you agree? Have some contemplative Christians withdrawn too much from the world?
7. Is it true that contemporary Christians seldom meditate?
8. What problems does a Christian encounter when he meditates?
9. Do you find moments of silence useful in corporate worship?
10. Do your prayers have a good balance of praise and petition?

Questions for Discussion

8 The Spirit Helps Us Pray

Prayer is a unique human activity, a different kind of approach to life. In prayer we acknowledge our great insufficiency and express our gratitude for God's concern. Sincere prayer is not, as some say, an escape mechanism, but a way of facing up to life's perplexities with divine assistance.

Much of our mental activity in prayer differs from that in the ordinary situations of life. Normally our experiences come through the physical senses, but in prayer the senses tend to be passive. In ordinary life we try to solve problems by reason, but in prayer we seek God's wisdom. In daily life we try to obtain the things we need by our own planning and efforts, but in prayer we seek help on the basis of divine grace. Normally we take credit for our achievements, but in prayer we praise God for His gifts to us.

When the Holy Spirit helps us pray, our prayers become, as Clement of Alexandria said, "a kind of divine, mutual, and reciprocal correspondence." Then our prayers are dialogues, a divine-human conversation in which we both speak to God and listen to Him, often receiving spiritual perceptions, insights, and intuitions.

Insight into Our Deeper Needs

We need the help of the Holy Spirit in our prayer lives because left to ourselves we do not know what prayers to offer or how to offer them (Rom. 8:26). Without the Spirit's guidance we often, like James and John on one occasion, do not know for what we are asking. Many of us recall unwise prayers we have prayed in the past, and we are now thankful God did not answer them.

Without the Spirit we do not know what to ask for because: (1) we do not know our own deeper needs; (2) we are unable to interpret critical life situations; and (3) we cannot see into the future. "Only the Spirit can teach us how we must pray," said John Bunyan. "Without the Spirit, though we had a thousand common prayer books yet we know not what we should pray for as we ought."

Our deeper personal needs. We have strong interior dispositions that hinder us from perceiving our deeper personal needs. Our desire for a favorable self-image causes us to overlook many of our faults and inner sins. We dislike taking a square look at ourselves because it often makes us feel inferior and guilty. Our psyches seek to suppress these feelings in various ways. The stingy Christian, a poor steward, rationalizes that he is simply conservative and prudent in his use of money. The hostile Christian sees himself as a man firm in his views. The resentful Christian simply represses his resentments because he feels more comfortable when they are concealed. All of us have tendencies to protect our self-images with ego armor.

Sometimes Christian motives obscure the insights of mature Christians. Holy aspirations may cause blindness to one's inner needs and failures. A church leader said that during the days of his administration, he was so zealous to see his area of the church prosper that he failed to perceive the deep needs of some who worked under his direction.

Our past experiences often hinder us from seeing ourselves as we are. A devout Christian said that in his youth he came to view himself as a good Christian because he kept a few religious rules; later, this bias made it difficult for him to see his deep interior needs. Sometimes we find that past traumatic experiences created so much anxiety in us that we fear to look back into those experiences, despite the fact that this would help us understand ourselves. Moreover, habits of thought and behavior, reinforced by repetition, shield us from personal insights.

We often fail to see our deeper spiritual needs because of our earthly desires and ambitions. James and John were unaware of their selfish ambitions when they asked for first place in the kingdom (Mark 10:35–45). The Laodicean Christians were so concerned with earthly prosperity that they said, "We need nothing," but the Spirit said that spiritually they were "wretched, pitiable, poor, blind, and naked" (Rev. 3:17). James told his readers that they had deep inner needs but that they did not even perceive or pray about them (James 4:1–3). He said that because their prayers were for earthly things alone, their prayers went unanswered: ". . . you ask wrongly, to spend it on your passions" (James 4:3).

The Holy Spirit helps us see our deeper needs by creating within us a desire for inner authenticity and diminishing the anxieties and tensions within us. He reduces our inner resistance to self-knowledge, readies us to carry out our roles in life without role playing, and strengthens us to give up our idealized self-images and our ego armor.

The Holy Spirit assists us to have insight into our deeper needs by lessening our desire for earthly things. Temporal values become secondary, eternal values primary. The Spirit creates within us deep longings for personal spiritual growth, and we pray for spiritual fulfillment instead of self-aggrandizement, for God's glory instead of self-enhancement. In such an atmosphere we come to see more deeply into ourselves.

The interpretation of life situations. In addition to our failure to see our deeper inner needs, we do not pray as we ought because we misinterpret life situations in which we are involved. Human dullness in perceiving spiritual factors in life situations is seen in the twelve disciples' inability to perceive the spiritual nature of the kingdom of God. They heard Jesus teach about the spiritual nature of the kingdom, but they did not understand because they had a preconceived idea of a restored earthly kingdom. Their wish for an earthly kingdom of Israel closed their minds to any other concept. Before Pentecost the disciples could not really pray for the coming of the kingdom because they did not know its nature.

All of us have limited spiritual perception of life situations because we have been trained to think in earthly concepts and rely on sensory experience. Often our spiritual perceptivity is dormant because seldom used. We need the Spirit's help to see the spiritual elements in our life situations, just as the twelve disciples needed the Spirit's revelation of the spiritual nature of the kingdom.

Surprises in the future. Furthermore, we do not know how to pray as we ought to pray because we cannot see into the future. "Do not boast about tomorrow, for you do not know what a day may bring forth" (Prov. 27:1). We must counteract the disposition to think that tomorrow's problem will necessarily be like today's, that today's wisdom will be adequate for tomorrow. The future often takes us by surprise, and unexpected, unexperienced situations defeat us. The writer of Ecclesiastes pictures the way in which new evil situations can do this: "Like fish which are taken in an evil net, and like birds which are caught in a snare, so the sons of men are snared at an evil time, when it suddenly falls upon them" (Eccles. 9:12).

On the evening before the crucifixion, the disciples of Jesus forsook Him because they were surprised at and unprepared for the turn of events. Earlier that evening Jesus had told them that they all would forsake Him, but they, filled with a sense of self-sufficiency, were confident that they would not. Peter even declared vehemently, "If I must die with you, I will not deny you" (Mark 14:31). His presumption soon disappeared, and as the unexpected events of the evening took place, he denied Christ. Peter found that his good intentions were not enough in an hour of trial.

Our inability to see into the future means that all of us are sailing on personally uncharted seas; we need a guide who knows the way. To change the figure of speech, the unknown future makes all of us amateurs in the matter of living; we need the Holy Spirit to teach us.

A Knowledge of God's Will

Every Christian needs the help of the Spirit to know God's will for himself. It is difficult for contemporary Christians to know God's will because our culture has a few shallow notions and superficial catchwords for it. Catchwords often conceal "monstrous perversions of truth," and half-truths usually cause us to neglect whole truths.

A knowledge of the divine will is basic to prayer for it prevents any futile efforts to overcome that will. "Prayer," Richard C. Trench said, "is not overcoming God's reluctance; it is laying hold of his highest willingness." Prayer becomes futile and harmful when we pray "Thy will be changed for me," when we ask selfishly that two plus two may equal five.

It becomes harmful because such petitions are not answered by a wise heavenly Father, and we begin to see prayer as ineffective. The heavenly Father must be grieved when we pray for things that are contrary to His will.

The character of God's will. The Holy Spirit helps us see that the will of God is founded in His love. This is seen in many places in the Bible, and it is explicit in the Greek term *thelēma,* which means "will" and is often used of God's will. The term has both rational and affectional elements, suggesting the love and desire that underlie God's will for us. His will comes from His gracious disposition. Perhaps nowhere does *thelēma* stand for God's arbitrary commands as such, but rather for God's fatherly purposes for us.[1]

The Holy Spirit helps us feel deeply that God's will is always good, as Paul said in Romans 8:28: "We know that in everything God works for good with those who love him, who are called according to his purpose." We come to understand that the holy character of God makes it impossible for Him to will that which is evil.

---

1. Hermann Cremer, *Biblico-Theological Lexicon of the New Testament,* trans. William Urwick, 4th ed. (Edinburgh: Clark, 1892), p. 728.

Positive attitudes toward God's will. The Holy Spirit enables us to perceive the divine will by giving us clear minds, honest hearts, and humble attitudes. He helps us have positive dispositions toward the divine will. The Spirit-filled Christian does not feel that the will of God calls for sad resignation. It is not an inscription on the tombstone of one's aspirations, but a call to fulfilled living. The Christian believes that a knowledge of God's will is the most valuable knowledge he can possess.

Positive attitudes toward God's will help us stop concentrating on our wishes and listen to God's wishes. We pray, "Speak, Lord, for your servant hears." Henry Drummond reportedly said that ninety percent of our difficulty in knowing God's will is our unwillingness to do it.

Ways to know God's will. The Spirit helps us perceive in the Bible God's wishes for us. Our minds are expectantly open to His desires, and we no longer fear the truth. We seek truth instead of fleeing from it; defense mechanisms become seeking mechanisms. The Bible ceases to be a book of commands; it becomes the guidebook of life.

Moreover, as Victor Hugo said, "God makes visible to men his will in events, an obscure text written in a mysterious language." The Holy Spirit enables us to see the hand of God in the things that happen about us. Sometimes He helps us see in them opportunities, at other times divine warnings.

Furthermore, the Spirit helps us perceive God's will as we interact with other Christians. Christian fellowship was basic in the lives of the early Christians, for their small-group meetings were times of enlightenment, of sharing their experiences with each other. Their reports of how God had led them through difficult situations often revealed the divine will to others who were in similar situations. Jesus assured His disciples that "where two or three are gathered in my name, there am I in the midst of them" (Matt. 18:20).

Finally, the Spirit of God helps us discern God's will by guiding our minds when they combine our knowledge of the Bible and of the past, our perceptions of the present, our aspirations and hopes, and much other psychic material, and come to insights into God's will. This method, founded in human mental activity, must be guided by the Spirit, or it will fail. When we use this method, we must consider our conclusions tentative until we are sure that the Spirit has guided us. We should say, "Lord, this looks 'right' to me, but I can only see it from one point of view; how does it look from heaven?"[2]

Conclusion

Andrew Murray called his great book on prayer, *With Christ in the School of Prayer.* Just as Jesus taught His twelve disciples in the "school of prayer," so the Holy Spirit teaches believers today. This school of prayer emphasizes both a basic knowledge of ourselves and of God and the actual practice of prayer. The curriculum is the teachings of Jesus and of the rest of Scripture. Students who do best in this school–as in all schools–are those who see most deeply into the subject they are studying and who put their knowledge into practice.

One of the reasons why Henri Frederic Amiel, a man of great devotion, grew in his prayer life was that he prayed. On one occasion he thanked God "for the hour of prayer that I have passed in thy presence. Thy will was clear to me; I measured my faults, counted my griefs, and felt thy goodness toward me. I realized my own nothingness; thou gavest me peace."[3]

Mechthild of Magdeburg grew in the way of prayer as she surveyed its personal results. Prayer, she said, "makes a sad heart joyful, a poor heart rich, a foolish heart wise, a faint heart bold, a sick heart well, a blind heart able to see, and a cold heart full of fire."[4]

---

2. Joseph Parker, *The People's Bible,* 25 vols. (New York: Funk and Wagnalls, 1892), 17:32.

3. In Anne Fremantle, ed., *The Protestant Mystics* (Boston: Little and Brown, 1964), p. 257.

4. In Friedrich Heiler, *Prayer: A Study in the History and Psychology of Religion,* ed. and trans. Samuel McComb (New York: Oxford, 1932), p. 112.

Questions for Discussion

1. There have been many definitions of *prayer.* How do you define it?
2. Some studies have shown that almost all people believe they have better-than-average insight into their own personalities. What does this say about human nature? Do some of our friends know us better in some respects than we know ourselves?
3. Perhaps few of us would say that the Spirit reveals to us future events. Would it help us if the Spirit did? How does God prepare us for the surprises of the future?
4. Do you think that every person uses defense mechanisms at times to protect himself from feeling inferior or guilty? Is this always bad?
5. Can you illustrate the statement that half-truths cause us to neglect whole truths?
6. Does the Holy Spirit always reveal God's will to us when we ask Him to?
7. Is God's will always rooted in His love?
8. What principles are important in using the Bible to determine God's will for us?
9. Many of us do not pray enough. Why? What can we do to increase the effectiveness of our prayer lives?

9 The Spirit Enables Us to Trust God

Only spiritually prepared persons trust God to answer their prayers. Trust does not spring from spiritually barren minds or cold hearts.

It arises instead out of a relationship between the Holy Spirit and the believer in which the Spirit helps us grasp truths that provide a solid basis for trust and then helps us have mental-emotive dispositions to trust our heavenly Father.

Knowing of God's Concern and Omnipresence

The intellectual grasp of God's concern and constant presence will do much to create within us the disposition and motivation to trust God. The concept that God is near us every moment helps us feel that He is available. Knowing that God is a gracious heavenly Father who is deeply concerned for every phase of our lives assures us of His help. A life of trust must have a solid intellectual basis; mere sentiment about God is not enough.

"Deep within every man," Soren Kierkegaard wrote, "there lies the dread of being alone in the world, forgotten by God, overlooked among the tremendous household of millions upon millions."[1] A well-grounded belief in a concerned, gracious God who is near us helps deliver us from this sense of cosmic isolation.

Biblical views of God. Our trust in God depends heavily on Biblical knowledge because the Bible is the basis for our theological beliefs. Our potential for trust is great if we have Biblical views of God; it is small if we are unacquainted with Biblical views.

The Spirit causes the Biblical concepts of divine omnipresence and concern to become deeply rooted and pervasive in each of our minds—more deeply rooted than concepts to which we give mere intellectual assent.

As these concepts pervade our minds, they create a mental readiness to trust God, giving a spontaneous aspect to our faith. Persons known for their faith have let the Spirit make dynamic the truths of God's nearness to men and His concern for them. These basic truths about God have often lain static in our minds and hearts, but the Spirit causes them to become dynamic. Like dry tinder, He sets

these truths aflame with His presence and makes them glow with new and deeper meanings.

In a fine figure of speech, the Old Testament pictures God seeking out His children to help them, taking the initiative when they are in trouble: "For the eyes of the Lord run to and fro throughout the whole earth, to show his might in behalf of those whose heart is blameless toward him" (II Chron. 16:9). Job said that God stayed by his side, seeing all his ways and counting his steps. David said during a time of great trouble, "The angel of the Lord encamps around those who fear him, and delivers them" (Ps. 34:7). Prayer was a dynamic force in David's life because he believed that "the eyes of the Lord are upon the righteous, and his ears are open unto their cry" (Ps. 34:15 KJV).

---

1. *The Journals of Soren Kierkegaard,* ed. and trans. Alexander Dru (New York: Harper, 1959), p. 129.

David said that "as a father pities his children, so the Lord pities those who fear him" (Ps. 103:13). Divine helpfulness is personalized because God "knows our frame"; it is sympathetic because "he remembers that we are dust" (Ps. 103:14).

It was the divine initiative that sent Jesus to earth to help and to save men; sinful earthlings had given Christ no invitation to come to their aid. In His work on earth, the Son of God took the initiative in helping people. He surprised the discouraged lame man who had lain many years at the pool of Beth-zatha by asking him, "Do you want to be healed?" (John 5:6). Christ amazed the widow of Nain—and the group of mourners—by stopping the funeral procession and raising her dead son to life (Luke 7:11–17).

The words of Jesus, more than anyone else's, emphasize the heavenly Father's concern for persons. He said that God clothes the grass of the field, "which today is alive and tomorrow is thrown into the oven. . . ." (Matt. 6:30). He said that God feeds the birds, not allowing a single sparrow, for example, to fall to the ground "without your Father's will" (Matt. 10:29). Jesus' point was that if God is this concerned about the lesser things of nature, how great must be His fatherly concern for men.

Paul had an unconquerable conviction "that in everything God works for good with those who love him, who are called according to his purpose" (Rom. 8:28). When God's righteous purposes are at stake and when His children need help, He does not stand on the sidelines, like some of us, but involves Himself in human predicaments.

Results of belief in the God of the Bible. Great personal benefits come to us as we believe deeply that the ever-present God is active in the world, giving attention to the most minute needs of His children. We no longer feel that we are in a lonely and hostile world, for a God of love is everywhere in it. We feel deeply that we dwell in a larger life than that bounded by the petty interests of this world,[2]

---

2. William James, *Varieties of Religious Experience* (London: Longmans and Green, 1902), p. 272.

that we are related to a friendly power who sustains all things.

We sense that there is a *sacred touch upon common things* when we really believe that God is everywhere present in His world. We view the universe as, in William Temple's words, a "sacred universe." The Christian recognizes a genuine spiritual hospitality in the world that creates in him a certain "at home" feeling on earth, for God is there. He can say, "This is my Father's world, and I can relate to him in it."

The Christian has a *sense of security* as he thinks about the divine presence near him and in him. He does not feel like a desolate orphan. He has a healthy sense of security in this life and, through faith in Christ, is secure for eternity. He is related to the Eternal who is unaffected by the flux of things. He feels secure because his trust is firmly grounded in the divine promises and other Biblical truth.

A sense of God's presence in the world makes spiritual values more real to us. Love is of greater value than earthly possessions, and godly contentment is worth more than bank accounts. Faith is one of the indispensable elements of life. It is our response to the divine initiative. We recognize that the "living Christ within us is the initiator and we are the respondents. All of our apparent initiative is already a response, a testimonial to his secret presence and working within us."[3]

Faith is a continuing matter because our lives are an "eternal becoming." The Christian believes that divine creativity continues in the hearts of believers. He knows "himself to be at one with the active world of Becoming, that deep and primal life of the All, from which our own life takes its rise."[4] The dynamic Spirit of God changes interior static conditions and corrects wrong situations. We become hopeful and expectant when we believe that we move forward with God's presence.

---

3. Thomas R. Kelly, *A Testament of Devotion,* 10th ed. (New York: Harper, 1941), p. 30.

4. Evelyn Underhill, *Mysticism* (London: Methuen, 1911), pp. 42, 43.

Knowing God Through Christ

You may ask, "How can I, as a Christian, come to know God better? What should I do now?" What many need to do most is to become better acquainted with Jesus Christ through reading the Gospels again. The Holy Spirit carrying on Christ's earthly ministry, interprets the Gospels for all believers. Jesus said that the Spirit "will teach you all things, and bring to your remembrance all that I have said to you" (John 14:26). We become acquainted with Christ through personally "reliving" the Gospels, and as we become acquainted with Him, we become acquainted with God. The Spirit uses with us the same curriculum that Jesus used with the original disciples to better acquaint them with God.

The incarnate ministry of Christ was not only for a privileged few who followed Him in Galilee; it is for all men everywhere and for all time. Jesus said that "heaven and earth shall pass away: but my words shall never pass away" (Mark 13:31 KJV). He said that "the words that I speak unto you, they are spirit, and they are life" (John 6:63 KJV). His wonderful works are always contemporary because He, as the indwelling Christ, continues His ministry to both the temporal and the spiritual needs of His children.

Sometimes we excuse our minimal knowledge of the Gospels and of Christ by comparing our situation unfavorably with those who saw and heard Him in Galilee. We may say, "I would have been a good follower of Jesus had I been able to hear Him speak and see His miracles." But we overlook the fact that Jesus did not permit His physical presence to compel people to receive His words. Thousands of people in Galilee and Judea were unmoved. Many in Capernaum, for instance, doubtless stopped for a few moments to listen with divided attention to Jesus and then hurried away to attend to worldly affairs. The reception of truth depends more on the condition of the hearer's mind than on exterior conditions.

Reliving the Gospels. The Holy Spirit helps us read the Gospels "existentially," using our whole personalities–our intellectual, affective, and volitional capacities. We make the words part of our interior lives.

The Spirit helps us identify with one of the original disciples when we see that his experience and needs were like ours. Then it seems as if Jesus is actually speaking to us, and this makes His words highly relevant.

The Holy Spirit helps us mentally interact with the Gospels. We may affirm the truth we see. We may answer relevant questions as if they had been asked of us. We may express astonishment at Jesus' wonderful works, as did certain people in Capernaum: "We never saw it on this fashion" (Mark 2:12 KJV). We too may wonder "at the gracious words which proceeded out of his mouth" (Luke 4:22).

The Spirit helps us grasp the spirit of the Gospels sometimes by leading us beyond the meaning of individual words. As letters are not the poem but only the symbols of thought, so the Biblical words are not God's total revelation. Deep truths lie back of the words. The meaning of the incarnation cannot be expressed in mere words. The words only point to a vast and incalculable divine concern for troubled men. The meaning of the cross of Christ cannot be expressed in words alone. Here too the words bear witness to God's unfathomable love for men. The Gospel message becomes much greater to us as the Spirit leads us into the spirit of the Gospels.

Acquaintance produces faith. The early disciples came to have an unconquerable faith in God because of their acquaintance with Christ. It should be recognized, however, that a study of the Gospels and other Biblical materials, under the tutelage of the Spirit, have produced the same results since the days of the apostles.

We must, however, have both the written Word and the Holy Spirit if we are to know God. Without the Spirit the deep truths of the Word are hidden from us (I Cor. 2:4–16). We see little truth in the Bible when we read it without His help because we tend to interpret it from the perspective of worldly concepts. Many people who have read the Bible have found it a closed book for this reason. On the other hand, it is equally hazardous to emphasize the Spirit's illumination to the neglect of the Bible itself. We shall travel an uncharted course into subjectivity if we seek acquaintance with God primarily through contemplation, prayer, and the exchange with friends of human views of God. Some Christian mystics underemphasized God's Word and went on tangents that had no Biblical support.

Being Disposed to Trust God

The Holy Spirit leads us through various experiences to a state of emotional readiness to trust God for answers to our prayers. New attitudes spring up because of His indwelling presence, and these too incline us to trust God. They give spontaneity to our faith. We shall look at two reciprocal feelings that the Spirit creates within us and that provide strong motives toward faith.

A sense of need. Man's sense of need for God is a primary factor in motivating him to seek and trust God.[5] Persons who see themselves as sufficient for life's problems see no need to trust God; those who see themselves as inadequate before God may trust Him.

The human race, born in sin, has strong interior impulses to feel self-sufficient. Theologians have long emphasized that this attitude of self-sufficiency is both prominent and serious. Dante put it first in his list of sins. Thomas Aquinas saw it as the basis of human rebellion against God.

The Holy Spirit helps us see our inadequacies and acquire an attitude of humility. Upon seeing God in a vision, Isaiah said, "Woe is me! for I am undone. . . ." (Isa. 6:5 KJV). When the Lord appointed Jeremiah to be a prophet, Jeremiah said, "Ah, Lord God, Behold I do not know how to speak, for I am only a youth" (Jer. 1:6). Peter said to Jesus, "Depart from me, for I am a sinful man, O Lord" (Luke 5:8).

---

5. Friedrich Schleiermacher, a philosopher and theologian, first emphasized—and perhaps overemphasized—the place of "a sense of need" in man's relationship with God. Since Schleiermacher's time many psychologists of religion have come to see value in this emphasis.

The divine presence still causes people to feel creaturely, needy, and humble, and at such times we can look realistically at ourselves—our egos and our supposed wisdom and strength. There can be no impulses to pretense in the presence of the omnipresent and omnipotent One.

Aspiration and hope. The Holy Spirit also leads us to trust God by creating within us aspirations for a better life. He does not leave us feeling physically deprived or spiritually desolate because He does not want us to adjust to mediocrity. He shows us the possibility of better things and kindles within us a deep desire to realize them.

The things to which a Christian aspires are primarily things that will enrich his interior life. An inward power incites him to spiritual progress; an inward impulse urges him to trust God for what he needs. Aspiration prepares the way for hope, which is a recognition that one's aspirations may be realized. Aspiration and hope are the "parents of virtues," the forerunners in a life of faith. They become the guiding images of life as they envision new goals and lead the way to Christian maturity.

Hope brings refreshment to life, blowing like a heavenly breeze through the discouragements of the human spirit. It challenges us to renewed action, like the sunrise that signals a new day. It brings vitality to our spiritual lives, from which repeated acts of faith may spring. John of the Cross translated Isaiah 40:31: "The saints that *hope* in God shall renew their strength; they shall take wings as the eagles; they shall fly and not faint. . . ." Hope is spiritually invigorating.

Aspiration and hope lead us along the pathway of life to the gate of faith. Aspiration starts us along this path, but it is soon joined by hope. When we finally come to the gate of faith itself, hope says, "Now is the time to believe."

Believing but Not Presuming

It is important for us to distinguish between presumption and faith so that we may follow the Spirit beyond the halfway house of presumption to a genuine trust in God. The human spirit, often lethargic in spiritual matters, tends to stop before reaching its final goal. On the other hand, a clear recognition of the differences between presumption and faith will help us understand why some of our prayers are not answered when we think we pray in faith. Such a recognition may save us from becoming disillusioned with the trustworthiness of God.

Presumption is a false "faith" that often appears genuine. Frequently it is a mental conclusion that God will help us in a life situation before we have determined God's will in the matter. Sometimes in the Old Testament the term *presumption* means "to go beforehand"; we are presumptuous when we run ahead of the revealed will of God. Presumption usually comes out of strong personal wishes; faith comes out of studying God's Word and interacting with God.

Presumption is often the optimistic conclusion of a sanguine person that "everything is going to be just fine." It sometimes results from the uncritical acceptance of this syllogism: "God is good; God dislikes seeing His children suffer; therefore God will not let me suffer." It sometimes results from a narrow and partial view of our life situations. More often, perhaps, it results from our thinking that we shall have the things we desire. Presumption may appear in the lives of sincere persons who are basically healthy from an emotional standpoint.

Presumption is related to false prophecy. False prophets in the Old Testament, for example, reported their own ideas as authentic messages from God; presumptuous people report that God will do certain things in their lives before they have a solid assurance that He will do them. Both false prophecy and presumption are human fabrications, human forgeries, offending and discrediting God. The Old Testament was severe with "the prophet who presumes to speak a word in my name which I have not commanded him to speak": he "shall die" (Deut. 18:20).

The Holy Spirit helps us avoid presumption by showing us that the human mind has a strong urge to "believe" what it wants to believe. The mind seeks to protect the self from threats and hardships, employing numerous escape and defense mechanisms to do this. Psychotherapists have accumulated a great deal of clinical evidence that people try to maintain favorable and self-enhancing views of their lives.

The Holy Spirit helps us avoid presumption by helping us identify our real needs. He shows us that some of our wants are trivial or even spiritually harmful. He increases our sensitivity to and perception of the enduring values of life. He enables us to see things from a Christian perspective.

The Spirit grants to us insight into God's will so that we may respond to Him in faith. He makes relevant Bible passages alive and luminous to us, as if the words had been spoken directly to us. He sometimes makes our prayers like a conversation with the heavenly Father, helping us discern the divine will as we "listen to His words." He also helps us discern the divine will as we converse with Christian friends.

The Spirit helps prepare the way for a genuine faith by enabling us to say with the psalmist, "I delight to do thy will, O my God; thy law is within my heart" (Ps. 40:8). In times of personal trouble and suffering, He helps us have some of the same spirit Jesus had when He prayed in Gethsemane: "Abba, Father, all things are possible to thee: remove this cup from me; yet not what I will, but what thou wilt" (Mark 14:36).

Conclusion

The Holy Spirit works in the subsoil of our lives to create a spiritual richness that will yield a life of trust. Jesus emphasized that faith springs from good soil. No man can compel himself to trust God; trust in God springs forth from the Spirit-prepared personality.

The Spirit creates within us hospitable attitudes toward the divine presence and spiritual values. We have warm and confident feelings toward our heavenly Father, who is always near us. A consciousness of God in our lives helps us perceive the spiritual things of life. The Spirit helps us appreciate fully Jesus Christ, and our greatest desire is for Him to be the Lord of our lives. Such views and feelings enable us to respond affirmatively to the Spirit as He leads us in the life of faith.

Moreover, the deep interior basis for faith includes a sense of spiritual realities. The Christian believes that he lives in a universe that is basically spiritual, for God sustains it and is active in it, working for the redemption and the welfare of persons. God is no deistic recluse living in some faraway corner of the universe, nonchalant about His children. His presence in the world makes eternal values glow with meaning, and faith seeks to realize these values.

Questions for Discussion

1. Saving faith includes two basic elements: commitment to and trust in Christ. How basic are these elements when we pray to God for daily blessings?
2. How important is the Word of God in the life of faith? See Rom. 10:17.
3. Why do some Christians have greater faith than others?
4. It is said sometimes that a Christian's faith may be conditioned by such factors as (1) his childhood experiences with trustworthy or untrustworthy people, (2) inborn temperamental tendencies, and (3) personal emotional adjustment. Do you think these factors are important in the matter of trusting God?
5. Can we always be sure that our "trust in God" is genuine faith and not presumption?
6. To what extent do we have little faith because we have little aspiration?
7. Is hope really a forerunner of faith? Are we likely to trust God for things for which we do not hope?
8. Consider individuals in the New Testament who exhibited great faith: the leper (Matt. 8:2), the centurion (Matt. 8:5–10), the ruler (Matt. 9:18), the blind man (Matt. 9:27–31), the many sick people (Matt. 14:34–36), the Syrophoenician woman (Matt. 15:21–28).
9. Consider some obstacles to faith: scoffers (John 9:23–25), unbelieving friends (Mark 5:35, 36), discouraging circumstances (Luke 5:18, 19), lack of sympathy from fellow believers (Matt. 15:21–28).
10. Faith is one of the gifts of the Spirit (I Cor. 12:9). Do you think that the Spirit still gives some Christians an unusual ability to trust God? In what sense is our faith always a "given" from God?

Part 3

The Holy Spirit Enables Us to Live Victoriously

10 The Spirit Fosters Our Christian Growth

We grow in the Christian life (1) as the Holy Spirit helps us perceive interior spiritual needs and (2) as we respond to Him in trusting God for grace to meet those needs. Ralph Waldo Emerson said that "perception is converted into character" when we actually do what we perceive we should do. In the Christian life, perception is converted into spiritual growth when we trust God for grace to help us with our recognized inadequacies.

Insight into self and trust in God enable us to grow both gradually and suddenly. We grow gradually as the Spirit's presence provides a warm interior spiritual climate that fosters growth, as the Spirit interprets divine truth to us and leads us in the ways of righteousness. The Spirit also helps us grow suddenly, and it is this type of growth to which we shall devote our attention in this chapter.

Spiritual growth, like personality growth generally, differs from physical growth in that the latter is almost always gradual. Much spiritual growth takes place by little (or great) forward leaps. We grow as we make "successful responses to successive challenges," as Arnold J. Toynbee said of the growth of civilizations. We grow rapidly if, when we fail Christ, we see clearly why, and if we then trust God to meet our inner needs. We often grow by leaps in both small and great crises of life.

We may perceive our inner spiritual needs when we read God's Word or when we hear it taught or preached. Insights into self may come during fellowship with other Christians or during moments of reflective solitude. They may come in times of temptation or of victory over temptation. They come often when the Spirit leads us into Christian tasks for which we feel inadequate, into new experiences that demand that we go beyond our old, habitual ways of doing things.

We make forward leaps toward maturity when, on the basis of personal insights, we open our lives to the power of God in trustful commitment. These acts of faith may be made at any time—when carrying on the ordinary affairs of life, when praying alone, when reading the Bible, or when worshiping in a group. The spiritually prepared heart may meet God at any place and at any time.

Responding in Self-Perception

To respond to God in self-perception is primarily to remain open to the conviction of the Holy Spirit. It is closely related to repentance.

The Bible emphasizes the importance of perceiving ourselves accurately: Isaiah viewed himself as "lost" and "unclean" (Isa. 6:1–5); Jeremiah felt immature and inadequate to do the will of God (Jer. 1:6); Peter exclaimed, ". . . I am a sinful man, O Lord" (Luke 5:8).

Jesus urged men to look at themselves. His personal interviews were invitations to insight. His public discourses were highly personalized words that focused attention on human attitudes, motives, and ideals. His parables were graphic word pictures that dealt with the motives and longings of men. His messages were mirrors into which He urged men to look and see themselves with understanding.

Paul urged the Corinthians to "examine yourselves, to see whether you are holding to your faith. Test yourselves. Do you not realize that Jesus Christ is in you—unless indeed you fail to meet the test" (II Cor. 13:5).

Human thinking about self-perception. The Bible is not alone in calling for self-perception. Socrates gave us the unforgettable dictum "Know yourself," and many philosophers have said that "the unexamined life is not worth living." Contemporary psychotherapists agree. Karen Horney emphasized the need for "an ever increasing awareness and understanding of ourselves."[1] Carl R. Rogers wrote that self-perception is "the most important aspect of human adjustment." According to Gordon W. Allport, "Integration . . . requires insight, a knowledge of one's own values, a clear picture of one's assets and liabilities. Psychotherapy and religion agree on this point."[2] Albert C. Outler, a psychologically oriented theologian, said that "growth toward the best can only follow knowledge of the worst. . . . It is only as a person, conscious of his disorder, comes to see, for himself, the shape of that disorder, and the psycho-dynamic patterns at work in his life, that he can come to a true knowledge of his actual situation, enabled to form an estimate of it."[3] Outler said that "the precondition of all cure and growth and maturation" is "to know oneself as one really is."[4]

Experience confirms the need for us to look squarely at our moral and spiritual inferiorities. A young professional woman, trained in the behavioral sciences, recently said: "I made no progress spiritually until I came to see myself. Before that I was always blaming those about me for my failures."

Problems of self-perception. All of us want to have a wholesome view of ourselves; all of us need healthy self-

---

1. *Neuroses and Human Growth* (New York: Norton, 1950), p. 15.

2. *The Individual and His Religion* (New York: Macmillan, 1950), p. 95.

3. *Psychotherapy and the Christian Message* (New York: Harper, 1954), p. 170.

4. Ibid.

esteem and a realistic self-confidence. Jesus emphasized this in the parable of the talents: the faithful servants succeeded because they had sufficient self-confidence, the unprofitable servant failed because he did not (Matt. 25:14–30).

But self-confidence can become exaggerated. James and John illustrated this when they boldly told Jesus that they were able to drink from the cup of suffering from which He was to drink. Their cowardice at the time of Jesus' betrayal showed how wrong were their views of themselves.

Sometimes we resist negative views of ourselves because of our *exaggerated fears of guilt feelings.* This is especially true of persons who were unable to handle guilt and failure in a constructive way in their youth, often repressing instead of resolving it. Some of these persons were reared in rigid and perfectionistic homes. Overly high standards made it inevitable that they would fail often, and they grew up with a chronic sense of guilt and anxiety. Many such persons become resistant to all criticism.

Opposition to a knowledge of personal deficiencies also arises often in persons whose *"need to be right"* has led them to adopt a perfectionistic pattern for their lives. They fear failure so much that they deny their weaknesses and compensate for their failures. The Pharisees in Jesus' time did this by observing certain religious rules punctiliously—they even tithed their garden vegetables, "mint and dill and cummin." They were compensating for their failures in the areas of "justice and mercy and faith" (Matt. 23:23, 24).

In addition, *earthly-mindedness* hinders self-perception. The twelve disciples were unable to perceive many of their own inner motives as long as they viewed the kingdom of God as an earthly realm. James and John, seeking the chief seats in the future kingdom, failed to perceive that they were more interested in ruling than in serving others (Mark 10:38–45). Jesus' parable of the rich fool suggests that worldly prosperity causes people to forget about the needs of their souls (Luke 12:16–21). He emphasized that the desire for earthly riches and pleasures crowds out spiritual concerns (Luke 8:14). The Laodicean Christians, who had prospered financially and thought they had "need of nothing," were in fact spiritually "wretched, pitiable, poor, blind, and naked" (Rev. 3:17 KJV).

The Spirit's assistance. We need the Holy Spirit to help us receive unfavorable insights about ourselves because of our strong inner dispositions to remain as we are. As homeostasis enables the body to maintain its normal condition, so dispositions in the human psyche motivate it to maintain habitual ways of thinking and acting.

The presence of the Holy Spirit in our lives provides a spiritual atmosphere that is favorable to accurate self-perception. We feel no need of personally parading in His presence, for we recognize that He knows us as we are. We can face our personal deficiencies without hypocrisy and self-defense.

The sense of the divine presence creates within us desires "to make a creative advance into maturity." We see that personal growth comes through increased self-knowledge. The Spirit helps us feel that truth about ourselves is a primary requisite of life.

The Spirit gives us a basic humility that makes possible a realistic self-image. He does away with the need for extravagant pride systems by giving us a firm confidence in God.

The Spirit led Peter, the one-time arrogant disciple, to write to his fellow Christians: "Clothe yourselves, all of you, with humility toward one another, for 'God opposes the proud, but gives grace to the humble' " (I Peter 5:5).

The Holy Spirit shows us that what we *are* is far more important than our reputations, that earthly recognition is transitory but spiritual things are eternal. We desire genuine selfhood. We recognize that as a mountain lake is fed by unseen springs, so fulfilled living springs out of inner sincerity.

Responding in Trustful Commitment

Every one of our God-given perceptions of inner needs is accompanied by an invitation to accept divine help. We may accept it and, as A. W. Tozer said in another connection, "enter the banquet hall, and sit down with the bold and avid souls who would not allow diffidence and unbelief to keep them from the feast. . . ." Or we may reject the divine invitation and remain hungry and cold "outside the banquet hall into which we have been warmly invited."[5]

Christian commitment is the dedication of our lives to Jesus Christ. It involves attachment to Christ and detachment from the sinful things of the world. It is an effort to make real the "spiritual imaginations" about our lives.

Commitment to God's will is basic in the Christian life. There is commitment when one is converted, a deeper commitment when one receives the fullness of the Spirit, and continuing commitment as one understands God's will more fully. Commitment is progressive; it is like a person walking—one of his feet is always moving forward.

Everyone must have the help of the Spirit to make deep spiritual commitments. We are too earthy and human to respond to God's call in our own strength. How does the Spirit of God help us?

The Spirit's help. In calling us to commitment, the Holy Spirit works in our whole personalities. He enlightens our minds and awakens constructive emotions so that we act with our total selves.

Jesus urged that we give *critical thought* to the matter of committing ourselves to him. Those who made ill-considered decisions to follow Him were not "fit for the kingdom of God" (Luke 9:57–62). Jesus could not use superficial followers. He urged people to think as hard before making spiritual commitments as they did before making business decisions: "For which of you, desiring to build a tower, does not first sit down and count the cost, whether he has enough to complete it?" (Luke 14:28).

The Spirit enables us to respond to Christ's call to commitment with deep intellectual conviction. He helps us look squarely at how we should invest our lives. He leads us to survey human needs around us and shows us how we can help meet those needs. As we consider new spiritual decisions, He helps us examine our attitudes and reconstruct them when they are wrong; He enables us to view these decisions from an eternal perspective.

---

5. *The Knowledge of the Holy* (New York: Harper, 1961), p. 98.

The Spirit gives thoughtful Christians a capacity for spiritual discretion. This is important, for some of our calls to Christian advancement come in the form of inward impressions. We must be guided in deciding whether these impressions are the authentic voice of the Spirit or whether they are human impulses. This is crucial when, for instance, young people answer a call to enter the Christian ministry.

The Holy Spirit uses *emotional elements* as he leads us to make deep commitments to God. The emotional elements in repentance strongly motivate the sinner to decide for Christ, and these same emotions strongly motivate Christians. In some sense, spiritual commitment is repentance in action.

It is helpful for us to recognize the importance of the Spirit's influence in the emotional, or affective, side of our lives. As observed earlier in this book, Paul listed three prominent characteristics of the kingdom of God, and two of them—peace and joy—are emotions (Rom. 14:17). The great apostle also enumerated nine fruits of the Spirit in Christians' lives, and the first four—love, joy, peace, and patience—are primarily affective (Gal. 5:22).

The emotive elements are sometimes more important in decisions than the rational. The most noble purpose of human emotions is to motivate the will to act courageously.

Our emotions do much in determining what we shall be and what we shall do. We tend to follow our emotions. We normally do the things first that we love to do.

The Holy Spirit creates within us positive feelings about the will of God, even if it seems difficult to us. These feelings help override our natural resistance to personal sacrifice. Positive Christian emotions have a power of attraction; they are impulses to action.

The Holy Spirit gives aspiring Christians a healthy enthusiasm for spiritual values that makes them personally courageous and dispels the spiritual apathy that seeks to possess them. Devotion to God is dull when the emotions are dull. Apathy is a seed bed for spiritual indifference and indecision, for being "neither cold nor hot" (Rev. 3:15, 16).

The will makes commitments readily when reason and emotion agree. When they do not agree, when there is a conflict between what is emotionally attractive and what appears to be reasonable, we must look to the Spirit for more help. He usually joins with reason, making the rationale compelling and diminishing the emotional resistance.

The constructive power of commitment. Personal commitment to a worthy cause is a powerful constructive force. Life grows in the direction of its loyal commitments.

Commitment unifies our lives as we set our priorities. We grasp worthy objectives and release unworthy ones. Commitment involves both attachment to the good and detachment from the evil. We cling to what is right as we acquire a healthy nonchalance toward spiritually irrelevant things and an inner resistance to sinful things.

The committed life always has "selective omissions" in it. "That law which impels the artist to achieve harmony in his composition by simply dropping out whatever jars, or suggests a discord," wrote William James, "rules also in the spiritual life."[6] James drew attention to the words of Robert Louis Stevenson: "To omit is the one art in literature. If I knew how to omit, I would ask for no other knowledge."[7]

Commitment to Christ reorganized radically the life of Paul. It caused him to cease persecuting the Christians, to give up his Pharisaical studies in the Jewish law, and to abandon his efforts to become a leader in Judaism. Having surrendered all of these interests, he was free to fulfill his commitment to Christ. He considered all that he had given up to be of little value in view of the "surpassing worth of knowing Christ Jesus my Lord" (Phil. 3:8).

Christian commitment requires personal identification with Jesus Christ. As we identify with him, we become disposed to interiorize His teachings and follow His way of life. Allport spoke of what results when, for example, a boy identifies with a baseball hero. In the boy's "fantasies he may feel that he is this hero. . . . he is attentive to every

---

6. *Varieties of Religious Experience* (New York: Longmans and Green, 1902), p. 290.

7. Ibid., p. 297.

detail: to his hero's manner of speech, to the neckties he wears, to his posture and gait. All these and other tokens of prowess the boy imitates."[8]

John R. Seeley pointed out that Jesus, in contrast to the philosophers of His day, used His friendship to reconstruct the lives of His adherents. Seeley said that psychologically speaking, the first step "toward fine dispositions" is for a man to form a strong personal attachment to an outstandingly good person. Then speaking of a man identifying with Jesus, Seeley said: "To worship such a person will be the best exercise in virtue that he can have. Let him vow obedience in life and death to such a person; let him mix and live with others who have made the same vow. He will have ever before his eyes what he himself may become. His heart will be stirred by new feelings, a new world will be gradually revealed to him, and more than this, a new self within his old self will make its presence felt. . . ."[9]

An attitude of loyalty to Christ leads us beyond sinful interests and trivia and helps us distinguish between temporal and eternal things.

Conclusion

The Holy Spirit reveals our spiritual needs to us as He helps us see ourselves from the divine perspective. Self-perception is the first condition for spiritual growth. We shall remain in spiritual mediocrity if we reject the Spirit's "invitations to personal insight."

But spiritual self-perception must not be a stopping place. If it is, we may spend our lives in futile self-justification or we may engage in a morbid type of penitence, feeling that God is somehow pleased with our masochistic personal attitudes. We must implement our self-perceptions. We must go on to deeper commitments to Christ as the Spirit renews us.

---

8. *Pattern and Growth of Personality* (New York: Holt, Rinehart, and Winston, 1961), p. 105.

9. *Ecce Homo* (Boston: Roberts, 1866), pp. 109, 110.

Commitment to Jesus Christ makes God's truth a powerful integrating and constructive force in our lives. It is the criterion by which all things are judged, the standard par excellence by which we should live.

Questions for Discussion

1. Do you believe that our "growth toward the best can only follow our knowledge of the worst"?
2. How important is the perception of ourselves in repentance?
3. Do you agree with Martin Luther that repentance should be a continuing and a lifelong experience for the Christian?
4. Is it true that our friends know us better in some areas of our lives than we know ourselves?
5. How well can we know ourselves through introspection? Can we be too introspective?
6. What are some of the defense mechanisms we use to conceal a true view of ourselves?
7. How may prayer be a means of self-perception?
8. Are our emotions generally more influential than our reason when we make spiritual decisions? How can we resist the influence of negative emotions?

11 The Spirit Enables Us to Witness

The early Christians were a new kind of people because they had the power of the Holy Spirit in their lives. He had brought about such revolutionary changes in them that they differed profoundly from both Jews and Gentiles. In the second century their contemporaries called them "the third race" because they were unlike all of the people about them.

The early Christians believed they had received a new revelation from God and that they should share it with all men. Seeing themselves as standing at the threshold of a new age, they sensed a responsibility to help bring in that new age. As "citizens of heaven," God had called them to form "colonies of heaven" on earth.

The last words of Jesus before His ascension were highly motivating to the earliest Christians: ". . . you shall receive power when the Holy Spirit has come upon you; and you shall be my witnesses in Jerusalem and in all Judea and Samaria and to the end of the earth" (Acts 1:8).

The early Christian concept of witnessing for Christ was deep and broad. Patterning their witnessing after that of

Jesus, they sought both to help needy people and to share Jesus' teachings in spoken words. This chapter treats these two basic methods of witnessing. It draws its material from the lives of the early Christians and emphasizes God's enablement of those Christians.

The Spirit's Enablements

In the Old Testament the Spirit of God came upon persons and empowered them to do special work. This bestowal of divine power foreshadowed the gifts of the Spirit in the New Testament. Let us observe briefly the general character of these gifts of power in the Old Testament.

Gifts of power in the Old Testament. The Spirit of God empowered persons to do a wide variety of tasks. He enabled: Bezalel to be a master craftsman of metals, so that he might "devise artistic designs" for the temple (Exod. 31:2–5); Joshua to lead the Israelites into the promised land after Moses' death (Josh. 1:1–9; Num. 27:18); Gideon to lead the armies of Israel (Judg. 7:1ff.); Samson to accomplish physical exploits (Judg. 14:6); Samuel and others to judge Israel wisely; Zerubbabel to rebuild the temple (Zech. 4:1ff.); and, most important of all, the prophets to reveal the will of God to the people.

The Old Testament emphasizes that human abilities are not sufficient to do God's work on earth; they must be supplemented by divine strength. We can accomplish God's work, "not by might, nor by power, but by my Spirit, says the Lord of hosts" (Zech. 4:6).

Gifts of power in the New Testament. In the Christian era, the Holy Spirit Himself is the heavenly Father's great gift to all believers. His indwelling presence in our hearts helps equip us to serve in the kingdom of God. He leads us into new depths of the Christian life, opens new spiritual resources to us, and energizes our whole personalities.

Moreover, the Holy Spirit bestows gifts of power upon Christians. In New Testament times it appears that He equipped every Christian to serve in the kingdom (Rom. 12:3–8); sometimes by bestowing a new ability, at other times by enhancing an existing ability (cf. Acts 1:8).

The Holy Spirit enabled the apostles to preach the Gospel convincingly, the New Testament prophets to receive God's revelations, and teachers to instruct others in established Christian truth. He gave to others the ability to work miracles, heal the sick, administer the affairs of Christian communities, and carry on a ministry of helpfulness (Rom. 12:3–8; I Cor. 12:1–31). Cyril of Jerusalem suggested that the Spirit produces in Christians a variety of fruitage: as the rain that descends from heaven and makes the earth to blossom, "shows white in the lily, red in the rose, purple in the violet and hyacinth, and clothes itself in forms so different as those of the date palm and vine, so the Holy Spirit, through himself, one and indivisible, distributes his grace as he wills."[1]

Our human frailty makes us dependent on the Holy Spirit's help. He must enable us to initiate generous acts of Christian aid, to enrich the lives of people. Without His guidance, we go from one spiritual blunder to another. We may give things to the poor in such a way as to impoverish their spirits. We may visit the sick and leave them as they were because we did not encourage them with the right words. We may minister to people and still leave their souls hungry for eternal truth.

The arrival of new forces of energy is apparent in those who have received the Holy Spirit. These new forces suddenly result in constructive Christian activities. Some persons who were formerly "weak" become "more than conquerors." Their lives become, as Madam Guyon said, lives of "spiritual fecundity."

Witnessing Through Compassionate Helpfulness

Jesus' ministry in Galilee was as broad as human need. After His ascension, His disciples launched into the same

1. In Henry B. Swete, *The Holy Spirit in the Ancient Church* (London: Macmillan, 1912), p. 202.

kind of ministry. They shared the spirit of their Master, who had come not to be served but to serve (Mark 10:45 NEB).

Concern for the poor. Some affluent Christians in Jerusalem immediately after Pentecost showed their concern for poor believers by feeding large numbers of them (Acts 4:32–35). Barnabas, for instance, sold a field and gave all the money to the apostles to feed the poor (Acts 4:36). These early incidents of caring for the poor became a distinctive practice among Christians.

The poor were often helped directly by individual Christians in the early centuries of the church. Aristides, writing in the second century, said that believers who lacked "an abundance of necessities" would fast for two or three days so that they could give food to needy Christians.

As time went by, the Christian church charged the deacons of local congregations to seek out those who needed help. The deacons, as the "eyes and ears" of the pastors, reported the names of those whom they found suffering, and congregational funds were then used to help them. The need for relief of the poor became colossal as local churches grew: in A.D. 250 the Christian community at Rome was supporting 1,500 people.

This kind of concern for the poor was a "new thing" in the world in which the early Christians lived. This spontaneous love in action was an effective witness for Christ to both recipients and observers. Tertullian, living about two hundred years after Christ, said, "It is our care for the helpless, our practice of lovingkindness, that brands us in the eyes of many of our opponents. 'Only look,' they say, 'look how they love one another.' "[2] Rome's last heathen emperor, Julian, saw that "these godless Galileans feed not only their own poor but ours; our poor lack our care."[3] Julian sought, without success, to deprive the Christians of this means of evangelism by trying to duplicate it in the old Roman religion.

---

2. In Adolf von Harnack, *The Mission and Expansion of Christianity in the First Three Centuries,* ed. and trans. James Moffatt, 2nd ed., 2 vols. (New York: Putnam's, 1908), 1:149.

3. Ibid., p. 162.

Concern for the sick. The apostles took seriously Jesus' command to "heal the sick. . . ." (Matt. 10:8). They went forth on the basis of Jesus' authority "to heal every disease and every infirmity" (Matt. 10:1).

The first specific apostolic act that Luke mentions after the day of Pentecost is the healing of the lame man (Acts 3:1–10), an act which indicated the concern of Christians for the infirm and sick.

The Holy Spirit granted some believers in the early church the gifts of healing and of working miracles (I Cor. 12:9, 10), gifts that apparently were used widely. By the time James wrote his epistle—perhaps about A.D. 80—it was a rather general practice for physically ill people to be prayed for and anointed with oil by the elders for physical healing (James 5:13–16).

The church of the early centuries became "the great infirmary or hospital of humanity." All physically ill and spiritually sick persons might seek help there, where "the bishops and pastors are the physicians, but only as servants of Christ, who is himself the physician of all souls."[4]

Christians during the early centuries of our era often helped sick people in plague-infected cities, from which the populace had fled in fear. According to Eusebius, people would abandon those who began to sicken (sometimes even family members), flee from their dearest friends, throw into the streets those who were half dead, and leave the dead unburied. The Christians, however, "visited the sick without fear, ministered to them assiduously, and served them for the sake of Christ." "They gave food to all" and buried the dead that were lying in the streets. Christians of all ranks took part in those rescue missions—"presbyters and deacons and people of the highest reputations." Many became infected with the plague and died, "transplanting the death of others, as it were, into themselves."[5]

Through such heroic demonstrations, Eusebius said, Christians showed themselves "to the heathen in the clearest

---

4. Ibid., p. 112.

5. *Ecclesiastical History,* trans. C. F. Cruse, 12th ed. (Philadelphia: Lippincott, 1869), 7.22.293, 294.

light. For the Christians were the only people who amid such terrible ills showed their fellow feeling and humanity by their actions. . . . When this became known, people glorified the Christians' God, confessed the Christians alone were truly pious and religious."[6]

Christian concern for the sick made a strong impression on the populace of the Roman Empire because it was a revolutionary idea. In those days religion was intended for healthy people and not for the sick. The deities sought the sound and the good to worship them. "The sick and the sinful, it was held, are a prey to the powers of darkness; let them see to the recovery of health by some means or other. . . ."[7] Celsus suggested that this was the cardinal difference between Christianity and the Greco-Roman religions.[8]

Witnessing with Words

The verbal witnessing of the early Christians was often in a context of Christian acts, some of them miraculous. In the days immediately after Pentecost, the apostles' verbal witnessing was frequently an explanation of a miracle performed in the name of Christ. The early Christians also emphasized that words of salvation should be substantiated by consistent Christian living.

Words and wondrous works. The Book of Acts says that the apostles did many "wonders and signs" (Acts 2:43 KJV). The phrase "wonders and signs" in the New Testament refers to miraculous works that manifest the power of God in order to authenticate both God's messengers and their message. Such works were basic to the verbal witnessing of the earliest Christians: the Book of Acts is called *Acts* of the Apostles, not *Words* of the Apostles.

---

6. Ibid., 9.8.
7. Harnack, *Expansion of Christianity,* 1:104.
8. In ibid., 1:104.

The miracles performed by the apostles prepared the minds of observers to consider seriously the message spoken by the apostles. After Pentecost "a sense of awe was everywhere, and many marvels and signs were brought about through the apostles" (Acts 2:43 NEB). Their awe suggests that many observers recognized that something sacred was happening. Many of them came to have open minds as they saw God at work in their midst.

In Samaria, where there was a deep prejudice against Jewish missionaries, Philip proclaimed Christ, "and the multitudes with one accord gave heed . . . when they heard him and saw the signs [miracles] which he did" (Acts 8:6).

The relationship between wonderful works and effective words of witnessing is an enduring one. While few Christians today claim they have worked miracles in the name of Christ, many report genuine answers to prayer, and such answers may move people to believe that the one who prayed is in touch with God and that his words have value.

Words and Christian character. Paul emphasized the importance of Christian character in the matter of verbal witnessing. He said to the Philippians: "Show yourselves guileless . . . children of God in a warped and crooked generation, in which you shine like stars in a dark world and proffer the word of life" (2:15 NEB). He wrote Titus: "Show yourself in all respects a model of good deeds, and in your teaching show integrity, gravity, and sound speech that cannot be censured, so that an opponent may be put to shame, having nothing evil to say of us" (2:7, 8).

The Epistle to Diognetus, written early in the Christian era, says that the conduct of believers "is wonderful, and admittedly beyond all expectations. . . . They live in the flesh, but they live not after the flesh. . . . They obey the established laws, but in their own lives they surpass the laws. . . . They love all men and are persecuted by all. . . . They are abused and they bless; they are insulted and they repay the insult with honor. They do good, and are persecuted as evil doers. . . . The Jews war against them as aliens; the Greeks persecute them, and yet they that hate them can state no ground for their enmity."[9] Such righteous living qualified these Christians, by the grace of God, to tell others of salvation in Christ.

Good character prepares the way for effective communication. People to whom we talk look for sincerity and integrity in us. Only the person who loves "his neighbor as himself" can really commend love to others as a way of life. Only Christians who have internalized Christian truth can witness effectively for Christ.

Few have spoken more incisively than Emerson about people whose words contradict their lives: "What you are stands over you the while, and thunders so that I cannot hear what you say to the contrary."

Conclusion

Christians who witness effectively do so not just by saying something religious but by their attitudes, their actions, and their words in general. A Christian's loyalty to Jesus Christ is an unassailable testimony to his Lord. Sometimes that loyalty results in martyrdom: the term *martyr* means "witness."

Contemporary Christians have numerous opportunities to minister to people who are mentally or physically distressed. People suffer in a variety of ways—from misfortunes, troubles, poverty, and sickness—and there are Christian ways of helping all of them.

Christians negate the gospel of Christ when they are unconcerned about human suffering. Leo Tolstoi said that in his earlier life he was unmoved and unconvinced by Christianity because Russian Christians did not manifest victorious attitudes about "poverty, illness, and death."[10] When Christians do demonstrate genuine concern for people in distress, however, this constitutes a powerful witness for Christ. A Christian act of helpfulness is sometimes worth a

---

9. 5:4–17.

10. *My Confession, My Religion, and The Gospel in Brief* (New York: Crowell, 1899), p. 48.

thousand Christian words. People are moved when they see the gospel of love in action.

Effective verbal witnessing takes place in spiritually dynamic lives. The most convincing words come from Christians who feel they have found a great spiritual treasure and who want to share it with others. Then the spiritual reality within the believer speaks to the spiritual hunger in the unbeliever. It is the redeemed who speak most effectively about redemption.

Questions for Discussion

1. Does the New Testament support the statement that the early Christians "were a new kind of people"? If so, how did they differ from their contemporaries?
2. How do Christians today differ from their unbelieving fellow men?
3. How does the Spirit enhance our abilities to witness for Christ?
4. Some Christians emphasize the gifts of the Spirit. Do you believe the Spirit still gives gifts to Christians? Can you support your answer from the New Testament?
5. Is there still a need for Christians to provide for poor people in view of the numerous social relief agencies?
6. Has the Christian church been deprived of an opportunity for witnessing inasmuch as secular organizations now provide most poverty relief?
7. Should one *always* pray for the divine healing of sick people? If not, then under what circumstances?
8. Do you think some people today have the gift of healing?
9. Have you known anyone personally who has been healed through prayer and faith in God?
10. The situation of people today is much different from that of people during the first three centuries of the Christian era. To what kinds of contemporary distress can Christians most readily minister?
11. Verbal witnessing sometimes seems ineffective. What are some good guidelines for Christians to follow in witnessing to unbelievers?

12 The Spirit Empowers Us Spiritually

The early Christians "out thought, out lived, and out died the world," said T. R. Glover in a memorable statement. They brought a different quality of life, a new moral excellence to the world. Paul said that their lives shone "like stars in a dark world" (Phil. 2:15 NEB).

Many of the early Christians had been religiously undisciplined Gentiles, morally "dead through . . . trespasses and sins" (Eph. 2:1). As children of disobedience, they had lived in the passions of the flesh and had followed the desires of the body and mind. They had been by nature the children of wrath (Eph. 2:2, 3). How can we account for such a change in human character and behavior?

The early Christians "out lived" the world because the Spirit of God was present in their lives. He had made them new creatures in Christ (II Cor. 5:17). They were God's "workmanship, created in Christ Jesus for good works. . . ." (Eph. 2:10).

This chapter will discuss four basic ways in which the Spirit enables us to live as Christians. He gives us (1) moral strength through a sense of divine forgiveness, (2) new dispositions through new birth, (3) spiritual cleansing, and (4) continuing strength to live godly lives in Christ Jesus. Each of these ways provides strong motivation to thought and action.

Strength Through Forgiveness

Some of us have not stressed enough the moral and spiritual dynamics of forgiveness. We have looked at divine forgiveness primarily as a way of balancing the moral ledger rather than as something that reaches into the present with moral and spiritual power.

A sense of divine forgiveness is a "most powerful stimulus to persistent goodness." In *The Pilgrim's Progress* the man who became Christian trudged along with a great burden of sin on his back as he fled the City of Destruction. When he came to the cross, he looked in faith to Christ and the burden rolled off his back. Freed of his heavy load of sin, Christian "gave three leaps for joy, and went on singing." John Bunyan's allegory here is true to life. Divine forgiveness releases psychic energy once used to carry a burden of guilt, for use in living constructively.

Freedom from guilt-motivated sins. A sense of guilt causes fear and anxiety, and they in turn cause more sin. A teen-age boy, let us suppose, feels guilty about stealing. Afraid that his deed will be discerned, he lies about it. Thus, one unforgiven sin brings forth another sin.

A sense of guilt causes a decrease of moral self-respect, and this makes it easier to sin. Every person puts himself in moral jeopardy when he compromises his self-image. Moral self-respect, by God's grace, is a first line of defense against sin.

Unforgiven sin dulls the human conscience so that it lets us do those things that it once censured. Morals become lax when the conscience becomes too lethargic to do its task.

From unforgiven and repressed sins spring many sinful motives. Paul Tournier pointed out that repressed guilt "leads to anger, rebellion, fear, anxiety, a deadening of the conscience, an increasing inability to recognize one's faults, and a growing dominance of aggressive tendencies."[1] It is axiomatic that consistent Christian conduct is impossible as long as such an inner fountain of guilt and sin exists.

Moral instruction is inadequate for one who has not been forgiven. Rollo May told of a guilt-ridden and anxious client who had received much moralistic advice from his friends. The client said that his friends had been "like people calling to a drowning man to swim, when they didn't know that under the water his hands and feet were tied." Divine forgiveness releases the bonds to our past sinful lives and frees us to live Christian lives by the grace of God.

New spiritual forces. Divine pardon brings about a spiritual atmosphere in which new spiritual forces appear and grow. These new forces are highly motivating in the Christian life.

One of these forces is an attitude of gratitude, gratitude for having been rescued. Jesus said that gratitude is a highly motivating element in the Christian life: the creditor who was forgiven a large debt loved more than the one who was forgiven a smaller one (Luke 7:40–43).

The grateful Christian possesses a keen sense of stewardship of his time, talents, and treasures. A middle-age businessman, after sensing the personal significance of divine forgiveness, said he was "under bond to serve Christ." The mystic Teresa said she was motivated in her Christian life by a "sense of an unpayable debt."

Moreover, the Spirit's removal of a sense of estrangement from God meets one of our deep needs. Carl R. Rogers said that a basic condition for personal growth is to feel *received* by another. God's acceptance is the greatest acceptance we can have. It gives us attitudes of sonship instead of servanthood (Rom. 8:14–17). We have a new spontaneity in doing His will.

Rudolf Otto said that the sense of sonship the Spirit gives is "the novelty, the uniqueness of Christianity." It reestablishes our true relationship to God and men, meets our deep need for filial relationships, satisfies our wistfulness for

---

1. *Guilt and Grace* (London: Hodder and Stoughton, 1962), p. 152.

the divine presence, and motivates us to obey our heavenly Father.

The removal of a sense of estrangement from our fellow men also strengthens our moral dispositions. Our unforgiven sins no longer make us defensive; we no longer fear counteraction. We feel deeply that we belong to one another, and we encourage a climate of mutual understanding and acceptance. We are inclined to forgive offending brothers, and we anticipate their forgiveness when we wrong them.

Furthermore, the sense of divine forgiveness makes us free, free to look into our past life, to engage in introspection without the debilitating effects of guilt and anxiety. It frees us from the need to justify ourselves through rationalization, denial, and projection. We can accept ourselves as having been saved by grace, and we can trust God because our hearts do not condemn us (I John 3:21).

A seminary student with high potential for leadership spent his first two years on campus "unnoticed" by both students and faculty. In his senior year he changed radically and became an outstanding student leader. He credited the change to a new and reinforced insight that, because God had accepted him, he should accept himself. He did this in a humble but profound way, and it freed him from many of the attitudes and inhibitions that had made him ineffective. It released him for service.

Strength Through New Birth

In the new birth, the Holy Spirit gives us a rich store of spiritual resources from which to draw in living the Christian life. He makes us new creatures in Christ, removing impediments to spiritual life and creating new spiritual capacities within us. We find a new readiness to do God's will, a new love of righteousness, and an increased spiritual energy that comes from the Spirit within us.

The moral and spiritual recovery that took place in the eighteenth century is due in part to an emphasis upon new birth. John Wesley, Jonathan Edwards, and others, in both England and America, stressed the deep sinfulness of human nature and the need for spiritual regeneration. Converts trusted Christ for salvation, and the changes in the lives of many were dramatically deep and quick. In Wesley's words: "The habitual drunkard, that was, is now temperate in all things. The whoremonger now flees fornication. He that stole steals no more, but works with his hands. He that cursed or swore, perhaps at every sentence, has now learned to serve the Lord with fear, and rejoice unto him with reverence. Those formerly enslaved to various habits of sin, are now brought to uniform habits of holiness. These are demonstrable facts. I can name the men, and their several places of abode."[2]

Paul said that one who has been reborn "is a new creation" (II Cor. 5:17). In another place Paul called the new birth a spiritual resurrection (Eph. 2:1ff.). Jesus said that the new birth is beyond human analysis but that we can observe its results (John 3:8); we can see that the lives of born-again believers are changed.

Renewal of the emotive-mental dispositions. The Holy Spirit transforms emotive-mental tendencies in believers—their sentiments, attitudes, and interests. "Regeneration is the primary reorganization of a person's entire motive life by the vital action and abiding presence of the Holy Spirit so that the ultimate motive is loyalty to Jesus Christ."[3]

Sentiments are organized systems of emotive-mental tendencies in reference to objects, ideas, and persons. They have been called both "intellectualized emotions" and "emotionalized thoughts." "A sentiment," Gordon W. Allport said, "is no mere static fitting of the mind, a simple storehouse for a cluster of related ideas and values. It is rather a mainspring of the individual's life from which radiate all manner of intentions whose purpose is to fulfill the values comprising the sentiment."[4] The Holy Spirit creates within our sentiments an increased love of spiritual values. Worldly things lose their excessive fascination, and spiritual things become more attractive and urgent.

---

2. *Works,* 14 vols (Grand Rapids: Zondervan, 1958–1959), 8:402.
3. Olin A. Curtis, *The Christian Faith* (New York: Eaton and Mains, 1905), p. 365.
4. *The Individual and His Religion* (New York: Macmillan, 1950), p. 126.

The Holy Spirit creates new *attitudes* in believers. Attitudes are interior tendencies toward action, a readiness to act, predispositions to behave in certain ways toward persons, objects, and ideas. Edwin D. Starbuck gave numerous instances of the radical change of attitudes in converts. One convert started to reconstruct his social relationships: "I spoke at once with the person with whom I had been angry." Another said: "I began to work for [i.e., to help] others." Still another said: "I felt everyone to be my friend."[5]

The Holy Spirit also creates new *interests* in believers. The new sentiments and attitudes become integrative centers for new interests. In this spiritual reorganization, some old interests are eliminated and replaced with new ones (II Cor. 5:17). The convert is "cold, callous, and blind" to sinful interests, "open, ready, and warm" to the things of the Spirit. The quality of one's life depends heavily upon one's interests. As a man "thinketh in his heart, so is he. . . ." (Prov. 23:7 KJV). Interests go far in determining one's personal goals and in forming one's habits. One man said, "Tell me a man's interests, and I shall tell you about his character."

Renewal of the mind. Jesus told His disciples, "To you it has been given to know the secrets of the kingdom of heaven. . . ." (Matt. 13:11). In contrast, He said of the unbelieving multitudes, ". . . seeing they do not see, and hearing they do not hear, nor do they understand" (Matt. 13:13). Paul said that our minds must be renewed if we are to know the will of God, if we are to know what is "good and acceptable and perfect"; he said that they can be renewed only by the Spirit of God (Rom. 12:2). The Christian's ability to understand spiritual things far transcends earthly wisdom, for we "have received . . . the Spirit which is from God, that we might understand the gifts bestowed on us by God" (I Cor. 2:12). Natural men, or unbelievers, cannot understand these spiritual truths, for they seem fool-

---

5. *Psychology of Religion* (New York: Scribners, n.d.), p. 127.

ish to them (I Cor. 2:14). Christians understand them because they "have the mind of Christ" (I Cor. 2:16).

The mind of Christ helps believers recognize the authentic voice of conscience when it, as Soren Kierkegaard said, "becomes merely one voice among many." It helps them know what is right "in the temporal order, in the unrest, in the noise, in the pressure of the mob, in the crowd, in the primeval forest of evasion."[6]

The Holy Spirit enables us to perceive clearly spiritual truth. This perception is necessary because we cannot respond to truths we do not perceive. We react hesitantly, or not at all, to the things we perceive dimly, while we may respond strongly to the things we see clearly and with vigor. Our response to Jesus Christ is conditioned by how clearly we see Christian truth.

Moreover, the Holy Spirit strengthens the volition so that it may will what is right. The Canons of Dort say that the Spirit "infuses new qualities into the will, which, though hitherto dead, he [now] quickens." The canons say further that though the will was "evil, disobedient, and refractory," the Spirit "renders it good, obedient, and pliable." He "actuates and strengthens it [the will], that like a good tree, it may bring forth the fruits of good actions."

Strength Through Spiritual Cleansing

God increases the strength of Spirit-filled believers by spiritual cleansing, purifying their thoughts, intentions, attitudes, sentiments, and interests. Spirit-filled Christians come to have a large degree of interior unity as the Spirit cleanses them of dispositions that are foreign and contrary to the Christian life. They are strong because they have less intrapsychic conflict. By the grace of God, they may say with Alfred Tennyson's Sir Galahad, "My strength is the strength of ten, because my heart is pure."

Spiritual cleansing, like the new birth, is a miraculous act of the Holy Spirit that we cannot completely analyze or

---

6. *Purity of Heart Is to Will One Thing* (New York: Harper, 1948), p. 186.

understand. The results of the Spirit's action in our lives are both broad and deep, extending into every area of our lives and reaching deep into our minds. The Spirit's presence is a purifying presence in the human heart, reaching into both the past and the present of our lives.

Spiritual cleansing was important in the lives of the apostles. Before Pentecost, Peter could not affirm that he loved Jesus with his whole heart (John 21:15–19); after Pentecost, he loved Christ so deeply that he suffered and finally died for his Lord. Before Pentecost, John had an ambivalent love of people, on one occasion asking that fire from heaven consume inhospitable Samaritans (Luke 9:51–56); after Pentecost, he ministered to the Samaritans, praying that they might have the same spiritual privileges as the Jews, and he became "the apostle of love." Peter said that the Holy Spirit's fullness in the disciples' hearts on Pentecost "cleansed" their hearts (Acts 15:9).

Cleansing the memory. The Holy Spirit cleanses the memory of believers, washing away the pollution of past spiritual failure and of guilt. This work of the Spirit is basic in the Christian life. Few things are more urgent than that we come to terms with our past lives.

The memory is a repository of the thoughts, emotional experiences, aspirations, and frustrations. Much of this psychic content is dynamic, and it does a great deal to determine how we react in the present. The storehouse of memory gives rise to wishes, tendencies, and dispositions. Henri Bergson once said that while we think with only a small part of our past, it is with our entire past "that we desire and will and act."

The Holy Spirit reaches into the past of every Christian believer and redeems the memory, making it a positive force in the Christian life. He causes us to lose our nostalgic feeling for our sinful ways. Like the prodigal son, we are so thankful for God's acceptance that we have no wish to return to a state of sinful impoverishment. The Spirit also cleanses from our memories feelings of enmity toward God, resulting in a deep desire to do our heavenly Father's will. He cleanses us also from the guilty fears that originated in our sinful pasts, and we, feeling accepted by God, serve Him out of devotion to Him, not to escape eternal punishment.

Cleansing from spiritual ambivalence. The Holy Spirit cleanses committed and trusting Christians from spiritual ambivalence, that is, from a love of God that is mixed with a love of the world, from a disparity between Christian sentiments and actions, from a love of some Christian truths and a dislike for others, from wanting to do both what God wills and what He does not, from being "mere admirers of Christ" rather than real followers of Him. Few words describe human nature better than *ambivalence.*

The Holy Spirit cleanses ambivalent Christian hearts by a gracious inflow of divine love: "God's love has been poured into our hearts through the Holy Spirit which has been given to us" (Rom. 5:5). God's presence in our hearts gives us a deep and genuine love of God, of other persons, and of spiritual things. This kind of love dispels contrary loves.

Thomas Chalmers emphasized the "expulsive power of a new affection." Love of Christ and of holy things expels the love of sinful things. This truth is axiomatic, for we can see it in both our lives and the lives of others. Love is the great integrating force in the Christian life, for it "binds everything together in perfect harmony" (Col. 3:14).

God's love in our hearts produces righteous living as it expels ambivalent tendencies. Augustine said, "Where love burgeons, there burgeons righteousness; where charity blossoms, there blossoms righteousness; abundance of love is abundance of righteousness."[7]

Spiritual cleansing has many facets. Thomas a Kempis and Jeremy Taylor saw primarily its rational elements and emphasized "purity of intention." Kierkegaard saw primarily its volitional elements and said, "Purity of heart is to will one thing." Wesley saw primarily its emotional elements and emphasized "perfect love."

All three are important dimensions of spiritual cleansing, and all help strengthen Spirit-filled Christians. Heart purity

---

7. In James Walsh, *Spirituality Through the Centuries* (New York: Kenedy, n.d.), p. 16.

is not a fragmented matter; it is not transient for the trusting Christian; it is not narrow and shallow. It is, rather, broad and deep, reaching into the whole personality of each fully commited Christian to strengthen him to do God's will.

Strength Through the Spirit's Presence

Ezekiel looked forward to the Christian age when, God promised, "I will put my spirit within you, and cause you to walk in my statutes, and ye shall keep my judgments and do them" (Ezek. 36:27 KJV).

On the evening before his death, Jesus said that the coming Holy Spirit would be to believers what Jesus had been—a helper or strengthener (John 14:16). The translators of the King James Version of the Bible used in this verse the word *comforter,* which in those days was closely related to the idea of strength. John Wycliffe used the word *strengthener.*

The last words Jesus spoke before His ascension were about the power of the Holy Spirit in the lives of believers: "But you shall receive power when the Holy Spirit has come upon you; and you shall be my witnesses in Jerusalem and in all Judea and Samaria and to the end of the earth" (Acts 1:8).

A central theme in Paul's teaching is that the Holy Spirit raises the Christian to a new level of moral power. Rufus Jones said that this happens at times by the Spirit "invading" the individual soul, as at Pentecost, and at other times by the soul breaking through all barriers and coming to the Spirit. According to the Canons of Dort, the work of the Holy Spirit in the human heart is "most powerful and at the same time most delightful, astonishing, mysterious, and ineffable." The Holy Spirit's presence means "a heightening of all human powers, the clarifying of human vision and judgment, the strengthening of the human will, and the discovery of latent and unsuspected possibilities of endurance."[8]

---

8. Henry Wheeler Robinson, *The Christian Experience of the Holy Spirit* (London: Nisbet, 1928), p. 41.

The presence of the Spirit in the Christian provides an *ethical spirituality,* a warm Christian climate in which righteousness flourishes. In such a climate, the Spirit gives us a vitality and sturdiness of life that go beyond our own resources.

The Holy Spirit helps us when both a sensual world and our own humanness would lead us astray through the imagination. Teresa said the imagination is "the fool of the house" that would lead us into evil. Paul said that "the peace of God . . . will keep guard over your hearts and your thoughts, in Christ Jesus" (Phil. 4:7 NEB) and that the Spirit will help us have ennobling thoughts (Phil. 4:8). A noble thought, like "intellectual passion," as Leonardo da Vinci said, "drives out sensuality."

The Holy Spirit brings strength in times of physical debility. Paul was strengthened by divine grace to triumph over his "thorn in the flesh." Paul prayed for deliverance from the affliction, but the risen Lord answered, "My grace is sufficient for you, for my power is made perfect in weakness" (II Cor. 12:9). Paul was contented with his situation, ". . . for when I am weak, then I am strong" (II Cor. 12:10). Here is an important Christian principle: Human weakness is the precursor of divine strength when it leads us to trust Christ for help.

Conclusion

Paul presents a compelling picture in Romans 7:7–25 of man's need of the Holy Spirit's help to live victoriously, although Paul does not here mention the Holy Spirit. The apostle tells of our failure to keep the moral law in our own strength. We "will what is right" but cannot do it; instead we perform the evil we do not wish to do (Rom. 7:18, 19).

The scene changes in Romans 8, where the Holy Spirit is mentioned at least twenty times. Human moral failure becomes victorious living in the Spirit. The "just requirements of the law" are fulfilled in us "who walk not according to the flesh but according to the Spirit" (Rom. 8:4).

There are no options to the help of the Spirit. Human ingenuity has been unable to find an acceptable substitute.

Moral education and discipline are unacceptable because they do not deal adequately with human perversity.

The work of the Holy Spirit is broad and deep in the lives of committed believers. He delivers us from the heavy drag of our guilty pasts and transforms our hearts radically. He cleanses us from sinful wishes and strengthens us to live victoriously in Christ.

Questions for Discussion

1. Is a sense of divine forgiveness "a most powerful stimulus to persistent goodness"? Why?
2. Why do people swear and blaspheme God? Is one reason their hostility to Him?
3. How important to Christian living is a sense of sonship with God? Do you agree that this is "the novelty, the uniqueness of Christianity"?
4. Do you believe in sudden conversion? In gradual conversion? In both?
5. How important are our sentiments in Christian living? How important are attitudes? How important are interests?
6. Do you believe that memories constitute a strong "push of the past"? Are unforgiven sins really a seed bed for more sins?
7. Give illustrations of spiritual ambivalence from the Bible, other Christian literature, or from your own life. Is spiritual ambivalence at the base of most Christian struggles?
8. What does Paul's expression "dead through trespasses and sins" mean?
9. What is our part in realizing the strength of the Spirit in our own lives?

Index of Authors